Woman's Mysteries of a Primitive People

The Ibibios of Southern Nigeria

by

D. Amaury Talbot

First published in 1915

Published by Left of Brain Books

Copyright © 2023 Left of Brain Books

ISBN 978-1-397-66804-2

First Edition

PUBLISHER'S PREFACE

About the Book

"This is an ethnography of the Iboibo, a Nigerian tribe. Written by a pioneering English woman in the early 20th Century, this book focuses on the ritual life of women. Despite the naive colonialist attitude, it presents a female perspective which was seldom seen in the ethnographic literature of the period."

(Quote from sacred-texts.com)

CONTENTS

INTRODUCTORY

FOR many years good fortune has granted to my sister and myself the happiness of living amid scenes of indescribable beauty and peoples of peculiar interest. The novelty of being the first white women to visit any particular spot has indeed long worn off by reason of the frequency of the experience, but the thrill of penetrating to places as yet unvisited by any European is still a matter of unmixed joy. Time and again our little party has been so fortunate as to happen upon peoples never studied before, who have been induced to confide to us traditions, beliefs, and legends of unexpected charm.

That all this came into our lives, a golden gift from the gods, without hardship worth the name, is due to the fact that, unlike Mary Kingsley and the small band of women travellers who followed in her footsteps, my sister and I were not alone. A never-failing watchful care has always surrounded us, smoothing each difficulty, and, as far as is humanly possible, providing against every discomfort and danger--at what cost of personal sacrifice one hardly dares to think.

During this time we were naturally anxious to do something in return for all that was done for us, and soon discovered that the chief way in which we could be of use was by making clear copies of rough notes jotted down in spare moments by my husband, and by writing out information which there was no time to collect save orally, thus putting upon paper page after page of description, incident or legend, which pressure of official work must otherwise have kept unrecorded.

When therefore a kind request came from England for a paper embodying "the woman's point of view" of scenes and happenings so different from those to which most of us are accustomed, the idea of separate authorship seemed to one who, up till then, had only acted as an unofficial secretary, almost as startling as if a pen from the inkstand had been asked to start writing on its own account. On thinking the matter over, however, it really appeared that, since the women of these regions had never yet been studied by a white woman, a paper dealing with the question from this side might have a certain interest.

It was not, however, until the mail brought a letter from one of the kindest and most brilliant literary men of our acquaintance, pointing out that, although men have taught us much of late years concerning primitive man, primitive woman is still unknown save through the medium of masculine influence, that the importance really struck us of making use of the chance which a kind fate had given us.

Only a few weeks before this letter was sent, Mr. Walter Heape, F.R.S., had written:

"From the biological point of view the crux of the whole matter lies in Dr. Frazer's convinced belief that the Central Australian women do not know anything of the part played by the father. . . . This is indeed a case when a woman's help would be of the greatest value. I venture to think it is not improbable a woman would have discovered something more from the female members of these Central Australian tribes."[1]

On this suggestion, therefore, and that of the friend already mentioned, we determined, in default of those better fitted for the task, to take up this branch of research. Yet, when we realised then for the first time that, for the friendly controversy at present waged between ethnologists--concerning exogamy, for instance-not one word of information is available from the woman's point of view, on a matter so nearly concerning her-- "without some man intervening either as inquirer or interpreter"--my sister and I seemed at a loss. We felt much as two sixteenth-century women might have done, who, hitherto following easily along paths made smooth for them by their men-folk, suddenly found themselves, at a turn of the road, standing alone--Nunez like--"Silent upon a peak in Darien," gazing out over the waves of an unknown ocean.

As is usual in such cases, once the study had been begun, difficulties, which at first loomed so large as to appear almost in the light of impossibilities, faded away of themselves. Although during the ten months of our sojourn among the Ibibios of Southern Nigeria, my sister and I were able to pick up but the merest fragment of the language, yet careful inquiry brought out the fact that a few native women in the district were capable of speaking intelligible English, and were willing, for a certain compensation, to act as interpreters. Among the Ibibios, surely, if anywhere, there is a chance to study primitive woman living to-day in all essentials as she lived, moved and had her being while Greece and Rome lay in the womb of Time.

This strange race, consisting of some three-quarters of a million souls, inhabits the south-eastern part of Southern Nigeria. Before our arrival in the Eket District, which forms the southernmost stretch of the Ibibio country, we had been informed, on all hands, that the natives of these regions were of the lowest possible type, entirely devoid of ethnological interest, and indeed, to quote the expression of our informant, "mere mud-fish." Saving the more civilised Efiks, it is indisputable that the Ibibios occupy a low rung on the ladder of culture, and are perhaps as bloodthirsty as any people throughout the length and breadth of the Dark Continent. Yet, to our minds at least, it would appear that their present condition is due to gradual descent from a very different state of things. Fragments of legend and half-forgotten ritual still survive to tell of times shrouded in the mists of antiquity, when the despised Ibibio of to-day was a different being, dwelling not amid the fog and swamp of fetishism, but upon the sunlit heights or a religious culture hardly less highly evolved perhaps than that of Ancient Egypt.

Indeed, if, as is held by so great an authority as Dr. Wallis Budge, much of the magic lore of Egypt may have originally come from the West, it is most probable that these very Ibibios formed a link in the long chain by which such knowledge was passed across the continent. In this case, the likeness in ritual or legend still occasionally to be traced between those of present-day West Coast tribes and of ancient Egypt would not appear to have been borrowed from the latter and borne across the Continent from east to west, but rather, contrariwise, from the Niger to the Nile. In any case, the Ibibios would seem to be a people of hoar antiquity, and so long have they dwelt in this region, that no legend of an earlier home can be traced among them.

By one of those strange coincidences which are always happening, it had come to our knowledge, some little time before the arrival of the letter asking us to undertake an independent study of the women, that here, at least, many customs of great ethnological interest still obtain which are not only unknown to men, but must always remain beyond the ken of male inquirers. For, by the unwritten law bequeathed to Ibibios from times so remote as to be almost forgotten, it is forbidden for any man to be allowed even a glimmering of mysteries which custom has decreed should be confided to women alone.

To mention one instance--when a man is slain in flight, only married women of his kin or town may bear the corpse to its last resting-place. There, in a part of the "bush" set aside for the purpose, and screened from all eyes, the last strange rites are carried out; but nothing that passes within those mysterious shadows may be revealed to man or maiden, whether white or black.

So much my husband had learned, and, as the matter seemed likely to prove of interest, I undertook further investigations, since it was probable that information denied him by ancient law might be given to me. After some difficulty, and on the promise that the name of my informant should never be given, an ancient woman consented to reveal to me rites surely as strange as any on earth. These will be dealt with more fully later, but it seems well to mention the matter here, because it was owing to this discovery that we first learned of the existence of the so-called "women's mysteries," and thus stumbled upon the knowledge that, in West Africa at least, and possibly among primitive peoples the world over, a vast field for research, untrodden as yet, lies open to women which to men must ever remain hopelessly barred.

On this point, Herr Gunter Tessmann, who was fortunate enough to witness the rites of the principal male secret societies among the Pangwe, writes in his excellent monograph: [2]

Die Schwierigkeiten, welche allgemein zu überwinden waren, ehe ich auch nur einen flüchtigen Einblick in das Kultwesen der Männer bekan, die sich auszudenken habe ich dem Leser überlassen. Hinsichtlich der Weiberkulte häuften sich diese

Schwierigkeiten eben durch den Ausschluss des männlichen Geschlechts und die natürliche Scheu der Frauen derart, dass es mir nicht möglich war, persönlich zu ihnen Zutritt zu erlangen." [3]

Since our eyes have been opened to the value of data collected from such women with no intervening male influence, it is a matter of deep regret to my sister and myself that we made no independent attempt on a former tour to learn the inner secrets of the great Ekoi cult of Nimm--the woman's secret society, which in the Oban District is strong enough to hold its own against the dreaded Egbo Club itself, and the secrets of which, though closed to all men, might, and probably would, have been revealed to us. It is the more unfortunate that, so far as we could learn, among Ibibio women only two exclusively feminine societies still exist, those of "Ebere" and "Iban Isong," both comparatively small and insignificant. The knowledge of what we had formerly missed, however, naturally made us the more anxious to lose no scrap of information which yet remains to be gleaned concerning those feminine mysteries which have survived to the present day.

In attempting to put upon paper some account of what was thus garnered, the first difficulty confronting so unpractised a writer, was to decide at which point of the life cycle to begin. At first we thought of starting this little study of primitive woman at the time when, as a tiny piccan, so fair as to seem almost white, an Ibibio girl-babe first opens her eyes upon the light. Soon, however, we found that the true beginning must be made still farther back. So far, indeed, that little more than a faint echo has floated down through the ages from those remote and distant times.

One evening my husband was seeking information as to the existence of sacrificial altars from a man belonging to the household of Chief Daniel Henshaw, who is head of one of the seven ruling families of Calabar and Native Political Agent for the Eket District. The man questioned on this particular evening was well known for his knowledge of secret things forgotten by, or hidden from, the common herd. He chanced to mention that the only case, in which, to his knowledge, altars were actually built, was on the occasion of sacrifices made to the Great Mother, Eka Abassi (Mother of God).

Offerings to this goddess are always laid upon altars built of logs set crosswise in alternate layers one above the other. When less than breast high, dry twigs are piled above, and upon these the body of a white hen is placed. This must be such a one as has laid many eggs, but by reason of age can lay no more. Fire is set to the twigs and the whole consumed, forming a burnt offering "sweet in the nostrils of Eka Abassi." Subsequent inquiries brought out the fact that the last-named deity is the mother not alone of the Thunder God, Obumo, whom we had hitherto been assured was the head of the whole Ibibio pantheon, but also of all created things.

From out the strange vague twilight of the gods therefore, beyond Obumo's self, looms, mystic and awful, the great dim figure of "The Mother"--recalling with startling vividness those dread presences met by Faust on his journey through the realms of the dead in search of the shade of Helen; the "Great Mothers," whose power was so vast as to overawe Mephisto-pheles himself--recalling, too, whole crowds of myths, lovely or awful, at the root of ancient religions. For Eka Abassi is at. once mother and spouse of Obumo, and between her and the other gods there is a great gulf fixed. To quote the Ibibio phrase, spoken in hushed accents, as was every mention of her--"She is not as the others. She it is who dwells on the other side of the wall."

Nameless, therefore, this Mother of gods and men looms, misty and vast, at the very fount of Ibibio religion. To none now living would the true name of the goddess appear to have been entrusted. Possibly only to a small band of initiates was it ever revealed, in accordance with the old belief that the names of supreme gods may only be confided to a chosen few, lest, by means of these dread names, men, and even lesser gods, might be tempted to conjure. Thus Ra explained the reason why the name given him by his great parents "remained hidden in my body since my birth, that no magician might acquire magic power over me." So Lilith, to avoid the consequences of disobedience to her husband Adam, is said to have uttered the "Most Great Name," by virtue of which she was enabled to flee away to a place of safe refuge, and indeed gained such power that even Jehovah Himself was unable to coerce her.

Eka Abassi may not be spoken of among the other gods because she is so far beyond them all. From her has sprung all which exists-from Abassi Obumo "the Thunderer," her son and consort, to the least of living things and every twig, stone or water-drop. In all there dwells some fraction of her. According to those to whom the esoteric teaching has been handed down from times when her cult was as yet unobscured by the fungus growth of fetish and juju worship which has since grown up to hide it, of her might be quoted the words, long hidden beneath the sands of Oxyrhynchus:

"Cleave the log and thou shalt find me. Break the stone, and there am I."

Perhaps most nearly of all does Eka Abassi manifest herself in the unhewn stones set amid sacred waters which are to be found scattered over the length and breadth of the land, or in the great trees, "the givers of babes." Her supreme attribute is "Bestower of Fertility," for, since from her all things have sprung, to her appointed dwelling-places creep barren women, to pray that their curse may be taken from them; while those with hearths left desolate by the silencing of lisping voices, lay before her curls clipped from dead heads, praying that the small feet may soon be set once more upon the earthward road to gladden the hearts of parents untimely deserted.

All babes born in this part of the world are sent by her; while, of the dead, save those who met a to violent end, men say "Eka Abassi has taken our brother."

Her eldest-born, Obumo "the Thunderer," once dwelt upon earth, but later went to join "the Sky People." Earth folk have lost the road by which he went, so cannot climb thither, but the Sky People sometimes, though rarely, come down to mix with the children of men. One such story is told of a family in Kwa Town, near to Calabar, who claim to be descendants of no earthly forbears.

"Long ago," so the legend runs, "a big play was being given. All the people were dancing and singing, when suddenly they noticed a stranger going up and down among them. He was very tall and splendid, but answered no word when questioned as to whence he came. All night long the festival lasted, and at dawn a strange woman was seen to have joined the guests. She, too, was finely made and beautiful, but sad looking, and, when asked of her town and parentage, kept silence for a time, but at length after much questioning said:

"'This "play" sounded too sweet in my ears, in the place where I dwelt on high; so I climbed down to hear it more clearly. Half way, the rope broke, and I fell. Now I can never go home any more, since there is no other way by which to climb thither--and I fear! I fear!'

"The townsfolk tried to comfort her, but she would not listen; only went up and down, wringing her hands and weeping. After a while, however, she saw the other stranger and, recognising him for a countryman, was comforted. He, too, had come down to view the 'play,' but had lost his road and could not go back. So lie set to work building a home for the Sky woman, where they two might dwell together. Later, children began to come to them 'softly, softly' (i.e. gradually and gently), and these were the ancestors of the present family."

* * * * *

In many ways the belief of Ibibio women as to the origin of the souls of their babes is much the same as that of Central Australians, whose theory, according to Sir James Frazer, is that a "spirit child has made its way into the mother from the nearest of those trees, rocks, water-pools or other natural features at which the spirits of the dead are waiting to be born again." That some such belief is held by Ibibios is clearly shown by the action of bereaved parents who, as already mentioned, bring curls, clipped from the heads of dead babes, to be placed in a hole in the rock, dedicated to Eka Abassi, here known as Abassi Isu Ma, i.e. "the goddess of the Face of Love"--or, since by a beautiful connection of thought the word for love and motherhood is the same, the name may also be translated "the Face of the Mother"--praying that she will speedily set the feet of their little ones upon the road back to life. In the sacred fish, too, with which all holy pools and streams abound, the souls of dead ancestors are thought to dwell, waiting for reincarnation. Unlike Central Australians, however, as reported by Sir James Frazer, Ibibio women--like their far-off sisters of Banks Island-- are well aware that without mortal father no earth-child can be born. Yet, while the body of the new-comer is clearly attributed to natural causes, its spirit is thought to be that of the "affinity," either animal or vegetable, with which one or other of its parents was mysteriously linked; or of an ancestor, returned to earth in this new guise.

Among those few, however, who still keep in their hearts, jealously guarded, the secret which has come down from times when woman, not man, was the dominant sex--that not Obumo, but Eka Abassi herself, is the great First Cause--one ancient crone was persuaded to explain to me, after considerable hesitation and obvious nervousness at the thought of confiding so intimate and sacred a matter to a stranger, that the laws which bind mortal women could not apply to the Great Mother of All.

"My grandmother once told me," she said, "that the Juju Isu Ndemm ("the Face of the Juju"), which lies in our town of Ndiya, is the mouthpiece of Eka Abassi. So great is the latter, that no husband was needed for the birth of her babes. By her own might alone, did the first of these, Obumo, spring forth; but to none of her descendants was this power transmitted. When, therefore, she saw that all the first earth-women were barren, long she pondered; then sent down to them a great white bird, which, on reaching earth, laid a gleaming egg--(the symbol of fertility).

"Old women tell that, after showing the people how, by honouring eggs and oval stones, and making sacrifice to the Great Mother, the gift of fruitfulness might be won, the magic bird flew back to its home in the sky; whence, with folded wings, soft brooding, she still watches over the children of men. Mortals call her 'Moon' and sometimes, when people are sleeping, the Moon-bird floats down from her place in the sky and pecks up grains or other food, which she finds lying about. She looks round to see that all is well with the earth-folk, and that the tabu on fowls and eggs is still observed; for in our town neither may be eaten, and, were this command broken, sudden death would fall upon the offender, by means of the great Juju Isu Ndemm. Should the hens have any complaint to make on this subject they would tell the Moon-bird, and she would bear their plaint before Eka Abassi, who would not only exact the death of the actual offenders, but withdraw her gift--thus sending barrenness upon all the countryside."

(It is because of this service that the goddess, as already mentioned, forbids the offering to her of any fowl, save such as has borne many eggs in its day, but, by reason of age, has ceased from bearing.)

The ancient woman naïvely added:

"That this is the simple truth and no fable, can be proved even to white people. For when you look up into the sky on a clear night, many or few, but plain to be seen, are the little star eggs-- and how could these get there, if it were not that the great white Moon-bird had laid them?

PRENATAL INFLUENCES AND BIRTH CUSTOMS

FOR Ibibio women motherhood is the crown of life, and therefore "jujus" thought to have the power of granting fertility or removing the curse of barrenness are held in greater reverence than all others.

Juju is beyond all else the force which dominates the lives of people such as these. The word itself is said to be taken from the French joujou, and was given to the fetish images everywhere seen because early traders of this nationality looked upon them as a kind of doll.

Many West-Coasters use the terms juju and fetish as if they were interchangeable, yet there would seem to be a distinct difference between the two. The latter appears to apply only to objects inhabited by the indwelling power of juju, which "includes all uncomprehended mysterious forces of Nature. These vary in importance from elementals so powerful as to hold almost the position of demi-gods, to the 'mana'--to use a Melanesian term--of herb, stone, or metal. In another sense the word also includes the means by which such forces may be controlled or influenced; secrets wrung from the deepest recesses of Nature by men wise above their fellows, or mercifully imparted to some favoured mortal by one or other of the deities." [4]

The word fetish is "derived through the Portuguese feitico from the Latin facticius--facere, i.e. to do. This shows the original conception at the root of the word." . . . . (It) "was probably first applied to images, idols or amulets made by hand, and later includes all objects possessing magical potency, i.e. bewitched or 'faked.'" [5]

Holy pools and rocks, many of which are regarded as the earthly manifestation of Eka Abassi, and are often connected with the rites of her son and spouse, Obumo the Thunderer, hold first place among jujus, in the opinion of the greater number of Ibibio women. True it is that her fame and glory have--save to a few initiates--long since been eclipsed by his. Yet "water, earth and stone, the three great 'Mothers,' are almost always to be found within the grove of the All-Father. Each of these is thought to symbolise a different phase of motherhood. The first, for instance, may perchance be taken as a representation of the Ibibio Aphrodite. She is all that is soft and alluring, while the fish which teem in her waters are the sign of boundless and inexhaustible fruitfulness. She never grows old or parched, neither may she be roughly used, burnt by fire, nor torn and cut by hoe and spade, as is the case with her homelier sister the Earth. This second member of the trilogy may perhaps be described as the working mother. She it is who produces the crops to nourish her children in life, and provides their last long resting-place when work is done." [6]

A term in common use for expressing the approach of death is to speak of the time "when my mother shall take me," because all men are laid to sleep in her gentle arms. It is for this reason, above all others, that Ibibios cling with such jealous tenacity to their land and so fiercely resent the least hint at a change of tenure. The proudest landowners of our own northern climes, who, at no matter what cost of poverty or hardship, hold to ancestral acres, can hardly be moved by so intense a passion at the thought of their loss as are these poor sons of the soil at the merest hint of a change in the land laws. Such a thought seems like outrage aimed at a loved one; for to them, Isong, the Earth Mother, is, in a way, nearest and dearest of all.

Stones and rocks again are also looked upon as givers of fertility; mostly in conjunction with Obumo himself. The genius of the stone is sometimes named Abassi Ma, and is looked upon in a special sense as the consort of the Thunder God. She it is who, more than all other manifestations of Eka Abassi, is thought to have the power to remove the curse of sterility from barren women, or send new babes to desolate hearths. It is naturally hard to induce primitive peoples to explain fundamental ideas such as these, yet, from what could be gleaned in the matter, it seems not over-fanciful to think that the trilogy of motherhood symbols may be taken to represent three aspects of womanhood--mistress, attracting and alluring; house-mother, drudge and provider; and consort, the sharer of dignities and honours.

Of the sacred pools, some two score in number, which we were privileged to be the first "white men" to view, that of Abassi Isu Ma, near Ikotobo--a rumour of which was first brought to my husband's notice by Mr. Eakin of the Kwa Ibo Mission, who, later on, induced a guide to lead us thither--is perhaps the most famous. In his company, one Sunday afternoon, we set out, and at length, after passing along a narrow path through thick "bush," reached the farthest point to which ordinary mortals had hitherto been allowed access. Beyond this only the head priest had been permitted to penetrate, in order to lay offerings within a hole in the sacred rock which faces the entrance and is the outward visible sign of the Great Mother herself.

"Low down on the face of the stone, beneath its veil of moss, and about a foot above the surface of the water, loomed a circular hole, partially filled by offerings laid there by the Chief Priest."

"A strange superstition has grown up around the rock. To it, or rather to the place of sacrifice just below, for, as has already been mentioned, the spot itself is too sacred for the near approach of ordinary mortals, come wedded couples to pray that babes may be born to them. Barrenness is regarded, not only as the greatest curse which can fall to the lot of man or woman, but also as a sign that the bride was a disobedient daughter. When a maid refuses to obey her mother, the latter says:

"'Because you have been a bad daughter to me no child shall be born to you, that thus atonement may be made for your undutiful behaviour.'" [7]

This idea is surely near of kin to the warning voiced in the "Maxims of Ani":

"Give thy mother no cause to be offended at thee, lest she lift up her hands to the god, who will surely hear her complaint and will punish thee." [8]

A little earlier in the same interesting document a man is bidden "to be most careful how he treats the mother who suckled him for three years and carried bread and beer to him every day when he was at school."

When an Ibibio woman has transgressed in such a manner, and punishment has in consequence befallen, her husband leads her down to the sacred pool. At the place of sacrifice they give offerings to the priest. Thence the woman wades up stream almost to the entrance of the sacred pool, where she makes obeisance and prays:

"O Abassi Ma! Keeper of souls! What have I done to anger Thee? Look upon me, for from the time I left the fatting-room in my mother's house I have never conceived, and am a reproach before all women. Behold! I bring gifts, and beg Thee to have pity upon me and give me a child. Grant but this prayer, and all my life I will be Thy servant!"

The priest then takes an earthen bowl, never before used, dips it into the sacred water, and pours some over the woman, who bends down so that face, arms and body may be laved by the stream.

When she rises again the little party climb up the steep bank to the place where the rest of the offerings lie. These are cooked and eaten by husband, wife and priest; after which the suppliant returns home, strong in the hope that Isu Ma will take away her reproach. . . . When a child is granted in answer to such a prayer, custom ordains that he or she shall be named 'Ma,'" [9] in gratitude to the Great Mother. This fact alone would appear sufficient refutation of the charge that love and gratitude play no part in West African religions.

So soon as an Ibibio woman discovers that she is about to bear a babe, old wise women of the race gather round her to teach the thousand and one things which she must or must not do in order to secure the well-being of the new-comer.

All over this part of the country grows a herb with blue flowers, the spikes of which bear blooms in shape like those of a giant heliotrope, but of vividest cobalt, while the stems look as if stained with indigo. The under sides of the leaves, too, are often blue veined, and, from a distance, stretches of this plant, which springs up upon old farm-land or any cleared space, look like a splash of summer sky caught in the green of the bush. Large posies of this flower are picked by the friends of the mother-to-be and rubbed over her body that her pains may be lightened.

The greater number of tabu imposed at such times relate to food. For instance, no snail, especially the great Acatina marginata, may be eaten, lest the babe should be afflicted with a too plentiful flow of saliva. Nor may an expectant mother eat pig, lest the skin of her child should become spotted in consequence, nor of the fat white maggots to be found in palm trees, lest its breathing powers should be affected. The tabu on pig, which is strictly observed here for mothers, is much like that reported from Guiana as imposed upon fathers, whose "partaking of the agouti would make the child meagre, or eating a labba would make the infant's mouth protrude like the labba's or make it spotted like the labba, which spots would ultimately become ulcers." [10] So far as could be learnt, however, an Ibibio father is not under the necessity of abstaining from any kind of food.

When a woman on the verge of motherhood chances to pass along a path crossed by a line of ants, she may not step over them, lest her unborn babe should be marked with a bald line round the head, supposed to resemble the "ant road." To avoid such a catastrophe she must first pick large leaves and lay these over the spot where she means to cross. Next she should collect sand and strew it over them, for only when the leaves are thus almost covered may she step across.

Mr. Elphinstone Dayrell informed us that among the natives of the Ikom District, of which he was Commissioner, the curious superstition obtains that should a man or woman chance to tread upon a millipede no further children would be born to them. Among Ibibios, too, these creatures axe regarded as the harbingers of misfortune.

Amid both Efiks and Ibibios the ancient custom still obtains that locks should be undone and knots untied in the house of a woman who is about to bear a babe, since all such are thought, by sympathetic magic, to retard delivery. A case was related of a jealous wife, who, on the advice of a witch doctor versed in the mysteries of her sex, hid a selection of padlocks beneath her garments, then went and sat down near the sick woman's door and surreptitiously turned the key in each. She had previously stolen an old waist-cloth from her rival, which she knotted so tightly over and over that it formed a ball, and, as an added precaution, she locked her fingers closely together and sat with crossed legs, exactly as did Juno Lucina of old when determined to prevent the birth of the infant Hercules.

Sir James Frazer, in the "Taboo" section of his wonderful book "The Golden Bough," gives many examples of similar beliefs. To quote a few instances:

"In north-western Argyllshire superstitious people used to open every lock in the house at childbirth. The old Roman custom of presenting women with a key as a symbol of an easy delivery perhaps points to the observance of a similar custom."

"Thus, among the Saxons of Transylvania, when a woman is in travail all knots on her garments are untied, because it is believed that this will facilitate her delivery, and with the same intention all the locks in the house, whether on doors or boxes, are unlocked." [11]

"The Lapps think that a lying-in woman should have no knot on her garments, because a knot would have the effect of making the delivery difficult and painful. In ancient India it was a rule to untie all knots in a house at the moment of childbirth. Roman religion required that women who took part in the rites of Juno Lucina, the Goddess of Childbirth, should have no knot tied on their persons." [12]

The temptation to quote from Sir James Frazer, which besets one at every turn, must, however, be resisted as far as possible, since, did one but yield to it, even to a comparatively small extent, such is the charm of style and vast learning of this great anthropologist that one could no longer venture to claim for this little record that it was written without intervening male influence."

*   *   *   *   *

Throughout the whole of her life no Ibibio woman may eat of a double yam or double plantain lest she bear twin children--the dread of which misfortune looms so large as to darken the existence of Ibibio women. Wretched indeed, in the old days, was the lot of any unfortunate mother of twins, since, though most of the men now deny this, averring that twin babes were only hated and feared as something monstrous and unnatural, a considerable number of women confessed that they, like those of many neigbbouring tribes, believed that one of the pair at least was no merely mortal offspring but that of some wandering demon.

Till a comparatively short time ago such a birth was followed by the death of both mother and babes, and, except where the fear of the white man is too strong, twins are not allowed to live even now. The custom is either to fling both little ones into the bush to be devoured by leopards or other fierce wood-folk, to offer them up on the beach to be eaten by vultures, or to kill one of them outright and starve the other, the bodies being then flung into bush or river.

Of late years this cruel custom has been modified to the extent that, after bringing about, or at least consenting to, the death of her babes, the woman is allowed to seek refuge in a town set apart for twin mothers. There she is still obliged to undergo "purification" for a period of twelve moons before being allowed to mix again with her fellows. In such circumstances it is customary, in some parts, for the husband to build a but for her and take food thither once a week.

On one occasion not very long ago a wretched twin mother, driven out of her town, made her way to the nearest "twin village." It happened that most of the inhabitants had almost "cleansed" themselves, that is to say, had passed through the greater part of the twelve moons during which they were forbidden to mix with their fellows. Contact with another woman who had but just borne twins would have rendered them unclean once more, so they drove forth the wretched mother, who, weak and almost despairing, managed to reach the town where Mr. Eakin, of the Kwa Ibo Mission, was staying at the time. The unfailing charity of this good friend provided all that was necessary for the moment; then, as soon as the woman was sufficiently recovered, they set out together for the nearest "twin town."

It was midnight when they arrived, and none of the inhabitants would open their doors to this sister in misfortune. So soon, however, as they understood that she was no longer alone, but accompanied by one whose word they had long since learned it was best to obey, a great clatter arose. A woman, whose time of "purification" was almost at an end, turned out every pot, pan and chattel from her dwelling, lest they might be contaminated by the new-comer, and bore them to the house of a neighbour whose year of seclusion was also all but over. The sick woman was then allowed to take possession of the deserted dwelling.

At stated intervals markets are held by the unhappy outcasts, to which, under certain restrictions and precautions, others may come to buy or sell. On the way to one of these markets, should a "twin woman" meet one not defiled like herself, she must spring into the bush and remain hidden till her more fortunate sister has passed by, so that the "clean" woman may not be soiled by contact with one so befouled. Perhaps one of the saddest effects of this cruel superstition is the dread with which "twin mothers" regard their own offspring. Mr. Eakin told us that once, on entering a house to which he had hastened on learning of the event which had just taken place there, he found a pair of new-born twins lying in a little basket. The wretched mother shook with fear whenever her glance fell upon them. It is difficult indeed to persuade such women to nourish their unfortunate babes, which are often only kept alive by the charity of Christian natives, or of women from other tribes who have come to settle in the neighbourhood. Such a case happened near Awa, in the western part of the district, where Mrs. Etete, a Christian woman from the Gold Coast, brought up to us twins and their mother, whom she had saved from death the year before.

Sad indeed is the lot of girl twins rescued from the fate ordained by the law of their race; for, unless some fortunate chance takes them away from their own country, they are shunned through life. No matter where they may strive to hide their secret it somehow gets known that they are "twin women," and no man would dream of approaching such with thoughts of love or marriage, save those who have absolutely no regard for their reputations. Only a short time ago a libel case was brought before my husband in one of the native courts. In this the plaintiff claimed heavy damages for defamation of character. During the course of the evidence it transpired that the words so bitterly resented had been--"He said that I was such a man as would be willing to marry a 'twin woman'!"

The gravity of this statement from the native point of view can readily be understood when one remembers that, by Ibibio law, any man found guilty of intercourse with a "twin woman" could be put to death. Even now it would be looked upon as sufficient cause for granting divorce to a wife if she could prove that her husband was keeping a "twin woman" as his sweetheart.

Also, should such a charge be proved against a member of the Idiong Society--one of the most powerful secret cults of the region--he was immediately expelled. On August 21st, 1913, a case in point was brought up before the Native Court at Ikotobo. In this, Ekkpo Akpan, son of the head priest of Idiong, stated on oath:

"The Idiong Society has a law that if any member should take a 'twin woman' as sweetheart he must be expelled. It was found out that Nwa Adiaha Udo Ide was a 'twin woman,' and therefore we decided that her husband should be turned out for having married her. In revenge for his expulsion the woman came and said that I also had been her sweetheart. She made this charge because my father is the head priest of Idiong, and she wished to be revenged upon him, through me. Formerly she had accused my brother of the same offence. The case was tried in this Court, and the members decided that her statement was false. Judgment was therefore given in my brother's favour."

With great difficulty and after much persuasion a woman of the tribe was induced to impart to me the secret reason which lies at the root of this dread of taking a girl twin in marriage. Shaking with fear at the thought of even mentioning so abhorrent a thing, my informant said in a voice so low as to be barely audible:

"Since the girl herself is not as other women, but part offspring of a demon, so the souls of children born to her go, sooner or later, to join their kindred, the evil devils. When the husband dies also, and comes to the ghost town, he finds the spirits of his accursed brood waiting to claim him as their father, and shame him in the sight of all the shades."

In this there would seem to be an echo of the ancient Babylonian and rabbinical belief "that a man might have children by allying himself with a demon, and although they would naturally not be visible to human beings, yet when that man was dying they would hover round his bed, and, after his death, would hail him as their father." [13]

No "twin mother" may pass through, or even near, a sacred water. This prohibition would seem also to apply to their offspring, but, as so few of these latter have hitherto been allowed to live, no case of actual transgression by them has come to our notice.

Once, in passing through the Okkobbor country near the town of Ube, we came to a little dell crossed by a raised path from the higher land beyond. On either side of the road was marshy ground, and, towards the middle of the glen, a stream of water flowed. right through the earth beneath the path.

We were looking at this and wondering how it had been formed, when a group of women and children passed by on their way back to Ube, their native town. When questioned about the water, they threw out their hands with the graceful gesture usual among this people in disclaiming knowledge, and answered, "Mi ifiokka," i.e. "I don't know."

It was quite obvious that they knew but would not tell. The prettiest and most richly dressed among them was wearing four silver bangles, each bearing the emblems of Faith, Hope and Charity; so her reason for disclaiming knowledge was easily read.

My husband asked if she were a Christian; whereon she at once, and proudly, answered in the affirmative. He then said, smiling and holding up an admonitory finger, "But Christians may not tell lies! "Whereon they all burst into laughter, and she began to speak:

"In the old old days long ago, a magic water lay between the little hills, and through this no 'twin woman' might pass. Mbiam Ube was the name of the spirit of the pool, and to him the people of Ube used to bring offerings of palm-wine and rum, white hens and black cocks; for this was a strong juju for the granting of prayers.

"One day there came a 'twin woman' who was proud and of a bad heart, and paid no heed to the old laws. Right through the water she walked, but it shrank away from the touch of her, and since then has only flowed through the earth, beneath the road, that it may no longer be polluted by the feet of such as she. To this day no one drinks of the stream lest he should die, but offerings are still made to the indwelling juju, for fear that he might otherwise grow angry and harm our town."

Fortunately missionary effort and the influence of white rule are now beginning to make headway against this dread of twins.

Once, near the end of our tour, on returning to Eket, the son of the head chief of a neighbouring town came to bring us the news that his wife and sister-in-law had each given birth to twins on the same day, only a few hours before our arrival. He is a Christian, and knew himself and his family secure in the protection of Government; but his dancing eyes and happy air showed that, in his case at least, the old horror of twins was a thing of the past.

How different were matters before the coming of white men, is proved by the fact that one of the first acts of the "African Association" after building their factory at Eket was to establish, on their own grounds, a place of refuge for "twin mothers." This afterwards grew into the Eket "twin town."

BIRTH CUSTOMS (CONTINUED)

THE rumour of another "twin town" of a very different kind has lately reached our ears. It is given on the authority of Akpan Abassi of Ndiya, who asserts that he visited the place with five companions. Certainly his fame as a magician has been greatly augmented since this visit. The following is his story:

"About three months' distance from Ndiya on the far side of the Kwa Ibo River, when one has journeyed past Opobo and past Bonny which lie to the leftward, after marching for many miles to the north-west, one comes at length to a part of the land where white rule is unknown. Here there is a town called Ekeple Ukim, where none but women live. It is a famous town, and the women who dwell there know 'plenty medicine too much.' That is why strangers go thither, because they seek to learn both magic and healing from its inhabitants. Our people call the place by another name, namely, Obio Iban-Iban, i.e. the Town of Women.

"By the side of the road grows high bush, which, as the town is neared, arches over till the view is quite shut out. So thick are the bushes, that towards the end of the way one cannot walk upright, but must bend down and in places even creep, especially where the bamboo clumps grow thick and high. When we had passed through this leafy tunnel, the prospect suddenly opened before us, and we saw the town, girt round with hundreds of giant cotton trees.

"Near to the main entrance bubbles a spring, the water of which is white like milk, because it flows over chalk. This the townswomen drink; but we refused it. Luckily, near by grew clumps of a cane, something like sugar-cane to look at, but with acid juice. This we cut and sucked, and its sap served us instead of water.

"When we entered the town the women left their occupations and ran up, crowding round us and asking by signs, 'What do you want?' Adding, 'No man may come here!'

"As we did not know the language of the country we could only talk by signs like deaf and dumb people at home. When we tried to explain why we had come, an old wife said further:

"'If you would live among us, even for a short time, each of you must sacrifice a fowl to our juju, otherwise you will die.'

"To this four of us agreed, but the other two said to themselves, 'What these people say is mere foolishness. We are strong and well, and have our own jujus; therefore we will not sacrifice to theirs.'

"On behalf of the four who made the offering ordained the women prayed to the gods of the town that their lives might be spared; and this prayer was granted. For a month all of us were permitted to stay because the women saw that we were foot-sore and weary, so they said that we might tarry for that space to refresh ourselves for the fatigues of the return journey. Longer than this we were not allowed to linger, so at the end of the time all six set forth once more; but the two who had refused to sacrifice died on the homeward way. Every day during our visit the women beat fu-fu and cooked soup, and set it out in a certain place. It seemed to be the custom for visitors to eat this, so we did so, and left money in exchange on the spot where the 'chop' had been found.

"At one place in this town was a great juju, the name of which we could not learn. On the top of it was a man's skull, and many skulls lay around. Hundreds of sheep and chickens wandered up and down in the streets, but not a single goat was to be seen, nor one solitary head of cattle.

"It was a very big town, and we wished to find out the reason why it was inhabited by women only. After a time we learnt as follows from nelghbouring tribes:

"'Once, long ago, at a town hereabouts, a woman bore twin children--a boy and a girl. Now, it was unlawful for twins, or the mother of twins, to dwell in these towns; so the inhabitants drove them off.

"'It happened that the husband of the woman loved her very much. So he said, "If my wife may not live in this place neither will I. I would rather dwell with her in the bush." He therefore followed her, and built a home where they might all live together.

In course of time the boy died, but the girl grew strong and big. Again the mother conceived, and bore twins once more, a boy and a girl. A second time the boy died and the girl lived. A third time also the same thing happened.

"'Now, all these girls grew up to be fine and tall, and when men passed by that way they wished to wed them. Each time, however, that a male babe was borne to any of these he died, and only girls were left. After awhile, therefore, the habit was formed of sending boy children away when they were still very small; while the girls remained and grew up, until at length they formed a big town. Even now, though they welcome lovers who please them, they will never let these stay for long. Boy babes are sent away to be brought up in the homes of their fathers, but girls must always remain with their mothers in Obio Iban-Iban.'"

Perhaps it is wrong to suspect our informant and his companions of other motives in visiting this mysterious town save that of the thirst for knowledge alleged by themselves. An air of retrospective pleasure ran through the man's account, however, possibly due to satisfaction in relating a rare--and indeed for this part of the world unique--experience. Unless my memory deceives me, certain similarities in his description and in that of the town of the Amazons given by Spruce in his book "A Botanist on the Orinoco," would, I think, strike the most casual reader. At any rate, the lot of these far-off "twin town" women is much to be envied by their unfortunate Ibibio sisters.

One day, when after a very long march we arrived at Okon Ekkpo, or Jamestown, as it is more usually called by white men, we learned from the two lady missionaries stationed there in connection with the Primitive Methodist Mission that an event, rare amid races such as these, had just taken place--namely the birth of triplets to a woman of the town. No sooner was news of this occurrence brought to the Institute than the devoted missionaries set out for the house of the unhappy mother in order to make sure that the new-born should not be sacrificed according to the ancient custom of the tribe. They found the woman in a state of utmost terror, and it was only through constant visiting, and themselves holding and tending the unwelcome new-comers, that the mother was somewhat reassured and induced to nourish her offspring. They noticed that one of the three was stronger and bigger than the others, and to this the mother devoted herself to the neglect of its fellows, which were therefore not long-lived. So far as we could learn this is the first case recorded among Ibibios in which even one out of a triple birth has been allowed to grow up.

To show how rare is such an event among primitive peoples, it may perhaps be well to mention here that among the Ekoi and neighbouring tribes, so far as we could learn, the arrival of triplets had never been heard of, nor would such an occurrence appear to be regarded as within the bounds of possibility. Dr. Mansfeld, a well known German Commissioner in the South Kamerun, told us that once, when questioning a native on the subject, the man had smiled with a superior air and answered:

"Aber, mein Herr, mit drei Kindern Niederkommen ist nicht möglich! Eine Frau hat ja nur zwei Brüste!"

Had it not been for the presence of the missionaries and a fear that rumours of the deed might reach the ever-open ear of Government, the mother and her three babes would, in all probability, have been sacrificed. The power for good wielded by such white women as these missionaries can hardly be exaggerated. Young, almost childlike in appearance, the one with wide-open blue eyes and long braids of golden hair falling below the waist, the other with eyes of steady brown set in a, face grown pale with overwork and strain, these two heroic women lived alone in a part of the district, which, although we personally have rather a partiality for it, is generally regarded as a kind of Alsatia for the whole region. The "Girls' Institute," for which at the time of the occurrence above related Miss Fisher and Miss Elkins had made themselves responsible, was founded some years ago by Miss Richardson, a member of the same mission, who later returned to resume charge of the education-al department, while Miss Fisher (now Mrs. Dodd) has accompanied her husband to another sphere of missionary work. To our pleasure Miss Elkins still remained.

In that part of the district which lies round Awa a reason is given for the killing of twins which is quite unconnected with any idea as to demoniacal origin. The following is the local account of the cause of the custom:

"The first pair of twins sent to Earth, so our mothers tell, unfortunately came to the dwelling of a family poor and of little account. When news of their arrival reached the neighbouring chiefs and members of great houses, these gathered together in much anxiety at such an unprecedented occurrence, and consulted as to what should be done. 'Behold,' said they, 'this woman first bore one child. Now she has given birth to two together; should she continue to go on in the way in which she has begun, next time she may bear four, and after that six or even eight, and so on until her family surpasses any of ours. If poor people are allowed to grow "strong" at such a rate, what will become of us? We shall have no chance to seize their property on the death of the head of their house, nor to force them to serve us as before when their family was small and of little account and there was none to take their part.'

That, so our grandmothers tell, is the reason why the murder of twins was started in the Awa country. Had the first twins come to a rich or powerful family there would have been no killing.

"Not long afterwards the king's head wife also gave birth to a boy and a girl, and a meeting of the townsfolk was called to discuss the matter. The king and his relatives tried their utmost to save the lives of the babes, but the poor folk combined and said, 'They shall be killed, as were those of our woman.' The more the rich strove to save the chief's twin children, the more did the poor insist upon their death, crying, 'As you did to us and our babes, so will we do also unto you and yours.' That is the reason why twin children were killed even unto our own day. In the country round Awa, however, no 'twin mother' is ever put to death, only driven forth from her town."

With this fear before their eyes, it is natural that women about to become mothers should consult a native doctor some time before the expected birth of their babes in order to learn from him if there is any probability of the arrival of twins. Should he answer in the affirmative, medicine is given by which the danger may be averted.

Next to the dread of becoming a mother of twins looms that of bearing a child into whose body some evil spirit has entered. This may be that of ancestor or kinsman undesirable on account of bodily or mental deformity, or because they come from a family tainted with "witchcraft."

So-called "birth-marks" seem to be quite common among this people, although such are here attributed to causes different from those assigned them in northern climes. An Ibibio baby is eagerly scanned for any sign which may reveal the identity of the indwelling Ego. Parents often notice some likeness to a dead friend, or trick of speech or movement in a child which to their minds shows that it is an old spirit reborn in some new body. A striking example of the way in which such deductions are made happened at Ndiya about ten years ago, and was told as follows:

"A man named Osim Essiet married a wife, and a little while before the birth of their first child he was attacked by an enemy and left lying in the bush with his head severed from his body. When he did not return, friends set out to look for him. After some time they found the corpse, bore it home and laid it upon a native bed. When the young wife saw this horrible sight, she cried out and flung herself down by the side of the body, calling upon the name of her husband and entreating him not to leave her.

"Some weeks afterwards the child was born. Round his neck was the mark as of a line at the place where his father's head had been severed, and, indeed, his neck is still shorter than that of most people. The townsfolk noticed this peculiarity, and felt sure, because of it, that the boy was really Osim Essiet himself come back to life again because he loved his wife very dearly and in answer to her entreaties that she might not be left alone. They therefore gave him, in his new incarnation, the same name as he had borne before."

A somewhat similar case happened at Ikott Atako, near Eket, and is thus related:

"There was once a woman of this town, Etuk Nkokk by name, who, not long after she had left the Fatting-house, bore a boy. At first the babe was like other children save that he was very weak, but as the years went on he hardly seemed to grow at all, and by the age of twenty was not quite four feet high. One day his mother went out and noticed the fine strong children born to her neighbours. When she came home, she looked loweringly at her sickly son and said, 'No other woman has a child like you! I wish you might die that I may be no more shamed by the sight of you!' Not long afterwards the boy sickened and died, and before they brought the coffin in which to lay him for burial the mother said to herself: 'This piccan gave me too much trouble!

I wish to find some way of punishing him and preventing him from returning to life.' So she took thought, and at length cut off his right hand, saying to herself, 'Now he will surely be ashamed, and not come back into my family any more.'

"A few months later another child was born, but lo! it was the same boy come back again, as was plain to be seen because he had only one hand. When the people went to see the mother and the new-born babe, they recognised him at once for the one who had died, and, seeing the handless wrist, asked 'How could you do such a cruel thing to your firstborn?' She answered, 'It was because I did not want him to come back again, and thought he would be ashamed to show himself among us thus maimed.' The people said, 'It is a misfortune, but it cannot be helped! This is your punishment, and you must just do your best for him.' So the woman took their advice and did everything possible for the child, in consequence of which he grew up and is still alive, a little taller than during his first earth-life, but smaller than other men."

The mother of Chief Henshaw of Oron regards him as an example of reincarnation. The name Nyung, by which he is everywhere known among black people, means "thrice born"-- an appellation which she gave him because her two first babes had died, and she believed that at his birth the same spirit came back once more; this time, not in vain.

The dread of the return of "wandering souls," who reincarnate only to bring trouble upon the family into which they have chosen to come, is common over the greater part of West Africa. Mary Kingsley thus describes the way in which parents seek to protect themselves against the infliction of these annoying spirits:

"When two babes in a family have previously died in suspicious circumstances the father takes the body of the third baby which has also died in the same way and smashes one of its leg bones before it is thrown away into the bush; for he knows he has got a wanderer soul--namely a sisa. . . . He just breaks the leg so as to warn the soul he is not a man to be trifled with, and will not have his family kept in a state of perpetual uproar and expense. It sometimes happens, however, in spite of this that when his fourth baby arrives that too goes off in convulsions. Thoroughly roused now, paterfamilias sternly takes a chopper, and chops that infant's remains extremely small, and it is scattered broadcast. Then he holds he has eliminated that sisa from his family.

"I am informed, however, that the fourth baby to arrive in a family afflicted by a sisa does not usually go off in convulsions, but that fairly frequently it is born lame, which shows that it is that wanderer soul back with its damaged leg."

Mothers seek eagerly for the first sign of resemblance to deceased relatives shown by a babe, and should no likeness be traceable, they watch to see which of the surrounding objects will first attract the notice of the new-comer. This custom is also recorded by Miss Kingsley in her characteristically lively manner.

"The new babies as they arrive in the family are shown a selection of small articles belonging to deceased members . . . .; the thing the child catches hold of identifies him. 'Why, he's Uncle John! See, he knows his own pipe;' or 'That's Cousin Emma! See, she knows her market calabash,' and so on."

AFFINITIES OR "BUSH SOULS"

THE time at which little ones first begin to creep must be an anxious one to those Ibibio mothers to whom no sign has as yet been vouchsafed as to the identity of the soul which has entered into their babes. For should the child be possessed by an "affinity," either animal or vegetable, the fact begins to manifest itself during the crawling stage.

The term "affinity" is in use among educated natives throughout the West Coast to express the mysterious link believed to exist between human beings and the plant or animal into which they are thought, under certain conditions, to have the power of sending forth their souls.

To white people, at first sight, such ideas seem so strange that it is almost inconceivable that they could have gained so firm a hold over the imagination of natives in such far distant parts of the world. When, however, we remember the belief in were-wolves and other terrible half-human folk, which persisted till comparatively lately in our own northern climes, the idea of the so-called Calabar "bush soul" becomes less incredible.

True it is that at home amid the matter-of-fact surroundings of the present day it seems, as one of our friends lately remarked, "impossible for human beings to believe that they actually take upon themselves animal form." Out here, however, whether camping in the vast dimness of the bush, or sitting, as now, in a little mud and wattle rest-house beneath which the dark, swift waters of the Cross River slip soundlessly by, such ideas take on a new aspect. The silence seems pregnant with mysteries, fascinating but terrible, the secrets of which, voices--half drowned in rustle of leaves or lap of water--seem ever about to reveal to the listening ear. For those, who live close to the heart of nature, there undoubtedly exists a link between man and the forest creatures, long since lost to dwellers in cities.

Even white men are, now and again, admitted to a strange intimacy with the jungle folk, and in some ways the uncanny tie, thought by some primitive peoples to exist between man and animal, seems hardly more strange than does the affection lavished by some bush creatures on those white intruders upon their solitudes into whose power chance may have caused them to fall. Once, at evening time, for instance, when sitting before our tents in a little clearing made in the heart of the bush, a tiny lemur sprang to shelter inside my husband's shirt from the snake or bush-cat which was chasing him. Months later, when the strange little beast lay down to die, as a result of a surfeit of coco-nut milk, after every conceivable remedy had been tried in vain, he cried like a baby on being abandoned because it was thought more merciful to leave him to die in peace; but settled down contentedly the moment one of us returned, and at length passed peacefully away, his tiny black-gloved hand clasped trustingly round one of our fingers. [14]

Again, there is the case of the splendid lion cub Fort Lamy, sent to us as a present from Ober-Leutnant von Raben, German Resident at Kusseri in the North Kamerun, with a letter in which the hope was somewhat quaintly expressed, "that the little lion might enjoy the ladies!" (presumably a translation of 'Die Damen erfreuen'). This beautiful creature, who, with his brother Kusseri, long welcomed visitors at the Zoo, was sent to England at about the age of six months, up to which time he had been constantly with us. A year's tour in Southern Nigeria and several months in England intervened before we were able to visit him. At last, one Sunday afternoon, we went with a friend. It was just before feeding time and the lion house was crowded, but Fort Lamy sat indifferent, alone in his cage, and with his back to the spectators. A single call, and he sprang to the bars--two great paws thrust through to clutch our hands, which he proceeded to drag inside, and stuff, with as much arm as he could manage, into his mouth. Then, still holding on, regardless of damaged gown or coat sleeve, the great beast flung himself upon his back and lay lashing the ground with his tail and exhibiting every sign of joy at meeting us once more. Perhaps natives would explain this unforgetting affection by saying that in past ages the spirit of the lion had been mysteriously linked with that of some mortal! Certain it is that for many years to come, the effort to disabuse the negro of his belief in "affinities" will prove useless. Hardly does one imagine that a little headway has been made in this direction than coincidence after coincidence happens to render the belief more deep-rooted than ever, and convince the black man of the mental blindness of the white in refusing to own even to the possibility of this and kindred subjects.

Then, too, the influence of dreams seems hardly to have been allowed sufficient weight as a factor in this and similar beliefs. In lands, where the dividing line between the so-called "real" and "unreal" shrinks to vanishing point; where water-sprites lurk beneath the surface of every pool or stream, and dryads flit through the shadows, visions of the night seem as real as the sights of waking hours.

To Primitive man the beasts are not, as to us, inferior creatures, but often superiors in force and cunning. The mystery and strength of huge, wise old elephants, the swiftness and force of the lion's spring, made these jungle folk objects of reverence, to be propitiated and, if possible, induced to act as patrons and protectors of the less powerfully built human denizens of the forest. In dreams the beasts play their part, beneficent or malignant, often, as with ourselves, changing and shifting shape; and primitive man made no distinction between sights seen awake or asleep. If he dreamed of a great snake or crocodile laying itself, bridgewise, across a stream, that he might pass over in safety, then it seemed to him that some such reptile must surely be the protector of his family, shielding it from danger as a father shields his children--possibly, therefore, the actual ancestor from which the tribe had sprung. To such men it must seem only natural to have the power of assuming the form of the brothers with whom they are mysteriously linked, and thus disguised sally forth as were-beasts, to snatch food in times of dearth, or wreak vengeance on an enemy.

A distinct likeness seems to exist between the present day "affinities" or "bush souls" of the West Coast and the idea which lay at the root of early Egyptian religion.

"Transmigration from one body to another, indeed, never presented any difficulty to the Egyptian mind. It could be effected by the magician by means of his spells; and there were stories, like the folk-tales of modern Europe, which told how the life and individuality of a man could pass into the bodies of animals and even into seeds and trees. The belief is common to most primitive peoples, and is doubtless due to the dreams in which the sleeper imagines himself possessed of some bodily form that is not his own.

"Egyptian orthodoxy found a ready way in which to explain the animal form of its gods. The soul, once freed from its earthly body, could assume whatever shape it chose, or, rather, could inhabit as long as it would whatever body it chose to enter. And what was true of the human soul was equally true of the gods . . . The soul of Ra, which was practically Ra himself, could appear under the form of a bird if so lie willed.

"It was only the cultivated classes to whom . . . the sacred
animals were symbols and embodiments of the deity rather
than the deity itself. The masses continued to be fetish
worshippers like the earlier inhabitants of the country from
whom most of them drew their descent . . . While the walls of
the temple were covered with pictures in which the gods were
represented in human or semi-human form, the inner shrine
which they served to surround and protect contained merely
the beast or bird in which the deity was believed to be
incarnated for the time." [15]

*   *   *   *   *

With regard to West Coast "affinities," many are thought to be
hereditary in families, but at times a babe is born to a house, no
member of which has ever before been known to bear the
"mark" of any animal, yet the likeness of some such can be
clearly discerned upon the new-comer.

The explanation for this was somewhat confusedly given me by
a woman, who herself had borne a babe belonging to the
baboon totem, although, as she sadly said, no "monkey soul"
had ever before been known in her family. The endeavour to
put into words ideas so mysterious and deep-rooted seemed to
cause a painful mental effort, and even the greatest care in
questioning left the matter still unclear. To those who have
never attempted such a thing, it is hard to realise the difficulty
of putting questions which will elicit the information which one
is seeking without giving any indication which might bias the
reply. It is of the utmost importance to avoid anything in the
nature of a leading question, since native good manners, like
those of old Ireland, necessitate a "pleasant answer," irrespective of veracity, should the least hint be given as to the
tendency of the reply desired. It would appear, however, that

the root idea of "affinities" is closely connected with totemism, but so near-linked in native thought with the belief in were-animals are both of these that the people seem incapable of making any clear distinction between the two.

My informant seemed to hold that the likeness to a baboon, clearly discernible in her son, though in no other member of the family on either side, so far as could be traced, was due to the fact that a "baboon soul" chanced to be awaiting reincarnation in the precincts of the sacred pool at the time when she went down thither to pray for the speedy coming of a babe. Under the term "baboon soul" she included both the ghost of a man who in a former existence had belonged to this totem, and of one who, during a long series of earth-lives, had been in the habit of sending out his soul into the form of a baboon "affinity," and so, by constant wearing of the were-shape his human body had gradually taken upon itself signs of likeness to its "affinity."

No very young child can send out its "bush soul." Only after about the age of ten years does the desire to do so begin to assert itself. Should the "affinity" be hereditary, the parents will be sure to notice signs of restlessness, and will then explain all that is necessary. Otherwise the "Drang"--to use a German word which gives the meaning of the Ibibio expression more nearly than any of our own--grows with the physical growth. First, in dreams, those possessed by animal souls see themselves wandering in were-form, and after awhile the desire to do so at will becomes so strong as to drive boy or girl to seek out someone to whom the secrets are known, in order to learn the rites necessary for the conscious taking on of animal shape. Afterwards they practise sending forth the soul into its were-body with ever increasing success, until they have at length acquired the power to bring this about at will.

Another way of becoming a member of an animal affinity is by purchase. This is usually brought about through negotiation with one of the Ekoi people, or some Kamerun tribe, among whom such strange secrets are said to have their home. These bought "affinities" will, however, be treated of in another place.

The most ordinary were-forms are those of leopards, crocodiles, snakes and fish. The following story was reported to Mr. Eakin of the Kwa Ibo Mission by one of his schoolboys named Etok Essien of Ikotobo:

"One day, a few years ago," he said, "I was sitting on the veranda of my house when I heard loud cries proceeding from another compound. I ran with others to the place whence the cries came, and saw a woman rocking to and fro, holding her hand to her throat and calling, 'I must die. I must die, for Akpan Nwan has shot me in the neck.'

"A crowd of people had gathered together, drawn like myself by the cries. Among them was a native doctor, who, at the woman's entreaty, cut open the place which she pointed out to him, and there, before us all, a lead bullet fell from it to the ground. When the woman was asked to explain how it came there, she said:

"'My soul dwells in a leopard, and, when I first cried out, Akpan Nwan shot this my 'affinity.'

"Enquiries were made, and it was found that the man mentioned had indeed shot at a leopard, which, at the very hour when the woman cried out, entered his compound to steal a goat. He: succeeded in hitting it in the neck, but it managed to escape to the bush."

Countless such stories might be quoted. We ourselves came across many people who claimed that, against their will, at certain seasons of the year their spirits went forth to wander in animal guise; but none was willing to own to consciously sending forth his soul, [16] because such a power is thought to savour of witchcraft. In every town, however, there are some inhabitants suspected by their fellows of using this uncanny power in order to wreak vengeance on enemies, or for the unlawful acquiring of riches. Many such instances were brought to our notice, and are recorded in another place.

Sometimes there is no outward sign to show that those with whom one lives in familiar intercourse are capable of projecting their bush souls in animal form. Such was the case of four children, the story of whom is thus told by Udaw Owudumo of Ikot Atako.

"There was once a man named Eka Ete, who had three sons and a daughter.

"One morning, very early, when the mimbo people [17] were going toward their grove to collect palm-wine, they saw four pythons hurriedly crossing the road. As usual the men were walking in single file, and, on seeing the snakes, the first ran back to his house to fetch a gun; begging his companions to watch the quarry meanwhile, so that it should not escape.

"On returning, he found that the pythons had only gone a little way into the bush. He therefore followed the tracks and soon overtook them. At once he lifted his gun and was about to fire, when the biggest snake raised his head from the ground and cried, with a man's voice:

"'Do not kill us. We are the children of Eka Ete.'

"The hunter did not fire, but lowered the gun and asked:

"'How is it possible for you to be his child, seeing that you are a snake?'

"To this the reptile answered, 'Go to our father, and ask for whatever you may wish of his in exchange for our lives, and he will give it to you.'

"Then the man left his friends to watch the strange quarry, and himself went back to the house of Eka Ete and said:

"'Awhile ago I saw four long snakes and wanted to kill them, but as I was about to do so one of them lifted up his head and said that they were all children of yours. Can you explain the matter?'

"On hearing this, the old man was very much astonished, and asked to be led to the place where the reptiles lay; for he had no knowledge of the strange power possessed by his children. No sooner did he arrive than all four lifted up their heads and cried to him:

"'Father! Father Save us! We are your children. Last night we came out, in snake form, and enjoyed ourselves so well that we paid no heed to time, and did not notice that day was dawning. When the sun rose we tried to hasten home, but the mimbo men found us while crossing the road, and since then they have watched us so that we cannot escape. Now we greatly fear that someone may kill us.'

"Eka Ete was quite confounded by what he had heard, but he called his people and set a guard about the snakes that none might harm them. Then he himself went to the Idiong diviner and asked:

"'How is it possible that these snakes can be the children who have hitherto dwelt with me in the house?'

"To this the priest of Idiong made answer, 'The souls of your three sons and of your daughter have of a truth gone forth in this form, and, should the snakes be killed, your children would die also.'

"On hearing this, Eka Ete asked, 'What can I do to make them come back home?' To which the Idiong man replied:

"'Get goats, fish, and palm oil, and offer these before the Juju Anyang. Should the spirit accept the offering, the souls of your children will be able to leave their snake form and come home once more.'

Eka Ete did as he was bidden; then waited anxiously to see what would happen. During all this time his four children had appeared languid and mazed, as though their spirits were wandering far away. About a week after the sacrifice had been offered according to the command of the Idiong priest the snakes crept back home during the night time: and after this the four children recovered, and became just as they had been before their souls went forth.

"When the father saw that all was well again. he was very glad and gave a great 'play' to all the countryside. Afterwards a feast was prepared with 'chop,' in plenty and much palm-wine, so that all the people rejoiced with him that the souls of his children had returned."

Another story of a "snake child," the likeness of whose "affinity" was plainly to be seen, was told us as follows:

"There was once a woman who bore a girl piccan. For many years she carried the child in her arms, because it could not walk, since it was a snake soul, and therefore had no strength in its feet. When this woman wanted to keep anything safe, she had only to set it upon a shelf or even leave it on the hob, for the child could not stand up to reach it.

"One day, before going to market, the mother cooked 'chop' and placed it, as usual, on the low mud wall by the fireside, so that it should be ready for her husband on his return from the bush. That evening when she came back she asked her daughter, 'Is my husband here?' And the girl answered No.'

"The mother went to see if the food had grown dry during her absence, but, when she looked, lo, there was nothing but an empty plate! So she asked:

"If my husband has not come back who can have taken his 'chop'? To this the girl answered, I do not know.'

"The woman was very angry, and accused other people in the compound of having stolen what she had so carefully prepared; but could learn nothing further.

"Another day the same thing happened, and this time she was even more vexed, and went all round the courtyard crying:

"'Who is it who comes to a person's house and steals the food which she keeps for her husband?'

"To this an old neighbour replied, 'I believe it is your child who cannot walk!' To which the mother answered:

"'From her birth my daughter has been unable to stand upon her feet. How then can she go and take things from the fireplace where I have set them?' Nevertheless she told her husband:

"'One old woman says perhaps it is our child who is the thief.' To which the man replied:

'Let us hide ourselves and watch.'

Next day, therefore, the woman bought a fine fish, cooked it very delicately, and set it in the usual place. Then she told her daughter that she was going to market. The husband had already gone out, and was hidden in a little outhouse built against the kitchen wall, through which a small spy-hole had been made. There his wife joined him.

Not long after they had settled themselves to watch, the girl who could not walk crawled into the veranda, and looked carefully round to see if anyone were in sight. Then she went all over the house to make sure that she was indeed alone, and afterwards, believing herself safe, came back into the kitchen. Suddenly she reared herself up till her head was high above the hearth, then easily lifted the 'chop' from the place where it stood, and sat down to enjoy it.

At once the parents ran in and caught her, crying:

'We did not know that it was you who did this thing. When the old woman told us, we would not believe her; but now we have trapped you ourselves.'

"Then the father beat his drum to summon the townsfolk, and when they came told them all that had chanced. In silence they listened to the story, then said:

"'Such a girl as this is not good to keep in the house.' The father answered, 'I think so myself. I will go and throw her in the river.' To which all present replied: 'Yes, that is the best thing to do.'

"So the man put the snake-girl into a canoe, and when they reached mid-stream threw her overboard. He then paddled back to the bank, where all the people were waiting, and watched to see what would happen.

"Not long afterwards they saw a very long snake come out of the water and creep into the bush. The father wanted to go after it and kill it, but his friends prevented him, saying: 'Do not go. Perhaps some harm might happen to you.'

"From that time onward no one saw either the snake or the girl again."

Beside "animal souls," the bodies of new-born children may be occupied by spirits of the great trees, such as camwood or cotton trees; or of climbing palms, lianes and even flowers. Among the Ibibios, however, we did not find so many, or so beautiful, legends of this nature as among the Ekoi of the Oban District--such, for instance, as "The Herb Daughters," "The Son of a Fruit," or "The Flower Child." [18]

As a general rule, only those belonging to the families of powerful chiefs can join the "affinity" of the great trees. The mother of one of the principal men of Afa Atai near Eket was thought to embody the "spirit" of a climbing palm; and at death her soul is said to have gone to dwell in a splendid specimen of this strange growth, which springs by a sacred water not far from the town. Thither, each year an offering is borne by her son, who consults her upon all points of difficulty, and obtains answers through the rustling of the leaves amid which her soul dwells.

Beside the power attributed to human beings of thus sending forth their souls into animal or vegetable form, accident brought to light the belief that some beasts are also thought capable of assuming another shape. For instance, when the anthropoid apes called by the natives "Idiokk" have grown so old and feeble that they know their end is near, it is asserted that they can renew their youth by sending forth their spirits into the bodies of new-born baboons, a species of which, for this reason, also bears the name of "Idiokk."

The discovery of this point, hitherto unknown, I believe, on the West Coast, illustrates the importance of taking down all available stories and legends, irrespective of whether or no such may appear interesting at first sight. It came to our knowledge through Udaw Owudumo, of Ikot Atako, who one day told us the following tale:

"Once a woman went to fetch vegetables for the evening meal. It was very near her time to become a mother, and, as she neared the farm, she felt that the babe was about to be born. She looked round and saw no one who might help her, so she prayed to her juju, saying, 'Let someone come to aid me and guide my piccan.' Yet no one came; only, just before the birth of the child, a very tall 'Idiokk' stepped forth out of the bush and said:

"'I will help you, and would gladly bear the piccan home for you, but fear that, should I do so, you would tell someone to kill me!'

"To this the woman answered, 'Only do as you say, and no one shall harm you.'

"So Idiokk aided her, and afterwards took the babe and they set forth together. As they drew near the house, Idiokk said:

"'Do not let us go by the front way, lest someone should see us. Rather let us enter by the back.'

"To this the woman agreed, and the beast went within and tended mother and babe. Then, when all was finished, he turned to the woman and said:

'If you will name this piccan after me, I will bring you as much "bush meat" as you need.' To which she answered, 'I agree'; and, on this account, the child was called Akpan Idiokk Ikot (i.e. Firstborn Baboon of the Bush).

"Morning and evening the ape killed 'beef' which he brought and laid before the door; then, entering, used to take the child from the arms of its mother and look sadly upon it. One day, while holding it thus, Idiokk said, gazing mournfully down:

"'I am sorry for you, because no stranger will cause your death. It is your father and mother alone who will bring this about!'

"That night, after the ape had gone, the woman's husband came home, and, finding the 'beef,' thought that it must be the gift of a lover, so asked jealously, 'Where did you get all this?'

"The wife answered, 'It is a strange beast named Idiokk who brings it.'

"On this the husband asked, 'If the Idiokk comes back again can I get a chance to kill him?' To which the woman replied:

"'Yes. He comes every morning and evening to bring me "beef."'"

"Next morning, when the poor ape came, he took the piccan in his arms as usual. Then the woman called softly to her husband who was hidden near by, 'Hist! He is here!' On which the man sprang forth armed with a cutlass to kill the great beast. At once the ape held out the babe to its mother that it might not be harmed, but the man slashed at the beast so cruelly that both ape and child died together."

Two or three days later the following story was told us by a native of Ikot Abia:

"There were many hunters in our town. One day a party of these killed a young baboon of the kind named Idiokk. This they brought back to the Egbo house, and sat down to skin it, after which they took some of the meat and cooked it before the fire. While they were doing this the Idiokk mother smelled the scent of roasting flesh from the bush and came out to learn what had befallen her piccan. When she saw what was being done, she drove all the people before her into the Egbo house, then snatched the remains of her son from off the fire, picking up meat, bones and skin, and carrying all away into the bush."

These baboons bear the same name as the great apes, because old men tell that the spirits of the latter can be born again in the shape of the former.

This belief seems to be confined to a very few old men in one part of the district. When Chief Henshaw was questioned on the subject he answered that no such idea had reached his ears, and continued:

"Also it seems to me contrary to reason, for, though it is well known that men have the power to send out their souls into the bodies of beasts, how can it be possible for animals to do such a thing, seeing that we are taught by the Bible that these have no souls? It is true that we see some creatures have the power to change the form of their bodies, as, for instance, caterpillars become butterflies and tadpoles frogs; but that great apes should send out their spirits to be reborn as lesser baboons I regard as a mere superstition of ignorant natives"!

A similar idea as to the power of some animals to transform themselves into other shapes is said to obtain among Malays, some of whom "refuse to eat the freshwater fish called Ikan Belidah on the plea that it was originally a cat. They declare that it squalls like a cat when harpooned, and that its bones are white and fine like a cat's hairs. Similarly the Ikan Tumuli is believed to be a human being who has been drowned in the river and the Ikan Kalul to be a monkey transformed. Some specially favoured observers have seen monkeys half through the process of metamorphosis--half monkey and half fish." [19]

CHILDHOOD

THE child cult is by no means so much in evidence among Ibibios as with the gentler natured Ekoi of the Oban District, where unkindness to little ones is practically unknown, and parents vie with one another in tender care of these small atoms of humanity. Yet even among the Ibibios, despite the almost ceaseless drudgery of their lives, the women at least seem never too weary to lavish care upon their little round-limbed brown piccans, and no single case of a neglectful mother has come to our notice.

Under these circumstances it is only natural that mother-love should prove deeper rooted than all else in the hearts of Ibibio children. A somewhat pathetic instance of this was shown by a murderer of seven years old, whose case came before my husband in the spring of 1913.

Two small boys were playing together, the one richly dowered with worldly goods, for he owned a clasp-knife and a piece of string, while the other, a child of poverty, had nothing. In course of time the poor boy chanced to lay predatory hands upon the string, whereon the capitalist, resenting this attack upon the rights of property, struck him a blow with the knife. As ill-luck would have it, the blade pierced straight through the heart, and the small victim fell back dead.

The relatives of the murdered lad came to the Commissioner demanding a life for a life, and the question as to the fate of the aggressor became a somewhat difficult one. In the end a missionary of great experience was persuaded to undertake the reformation of the little malefactor, who chanced to be brought to him on May 24th, when the principal chiefs and people of the District had been gathered together for Empire Day celebrations.

The small criminal walked quietly up to his new friend, and in a voice low, but strangely pleading, begged leave to go back to his town, and bid a last good-bye to the mother he had left.

"Why?" asked the puzzled missionary. "Did you not do so before you came?"

"I did," answered the boy, "but then we thought only that I was to be separated from her by a few miles. Now, I see clearly, from the crowd which is gathered here, that the people have come together to see me die, so I beg to be allowed to go back once again to say good-bye, since afterwards I may never see her more."

Such an attitude is typical of the race. It is seldom that one of this people attempts to struggle against destiny, should the odds be overwhelmingly heavy. Rather, they seem soberly to acquiesce in the inevitable, meeting fate with the stoicism of despair, which often lends them unexpected dignity and courage when face to face with death.

As a general rule fathers, too, seem to treat their offspring kindly, though, unfortunately, cases of cruelty to children are not infrequent. Two instances, which happened within a few days of one another may be cited as typical.

In the first case the husband was incensed against his wife, whom he suspected of infidelity, though without proof. After brutally maltreating the woman, he broke their baby's thighs as a means of still further punishing her. In the second, the little one, who had just begun to toddle, was pushed on to the fire by its father, with like intent.

The first ornament given to a baby is a string of beads tied round the waist, and, a little later, it may possibly be further adorned by the addition of a snail shell, thought to possess magical properties, which is suspended round the neck.

In many ways the lot of small brown piccans born in these climes is an enviable one, in comparison at least with that of the children of our own poor. Ibibio babies are almost always well nourished, and roll and creep contentedly enough in the warm sand, playing together like a happy litter of little bush cubs. They take considerable part, too, in the life of their elders, proudly riding to market astride the hip of a busy mother, safe girdled in the curve of her arm.

At an incredibly early age these little folk begin to take notice of what is going on around them, crawling out at the sound of the tom-tom, or striving to follow the "plays" given by their elders.

In every Oron town there is a young men's society, the name of which is Ekung. The avowed purpose of the ceremony is to bring more children to the town. It was thus described to us by Chief Henshaw:

"At the beginning of the dry season, after the feast of the new yams, a great 'play' is given by this society, to which boys and girls of the town come robed in their best. For days beforehand little maids cry to their mothers, 'We must have fresh dresses for the Ekung play,' while the boys also beg for new singlets, shirts and loin cloths.

"On this occasion one woman vies with another as to who can lavish most care upon the children. Each daughter's hair is elaborately dressed. Anklets and bracelets are slipped over feet and hands, and even the Fatting-house girls are allowed to come out and join in the celebration.

"When the 'Image' is seen approaching, with the drummers going before, young boys pour out to meet him, singing also and rejoicing. Some run in front, some behind, some on either hand--shouting for joy. Little crawlers, who had never walked, try to follow when Ekung passes. The mothers would stop them but cannot, so eager are they. Thus little ones often walk for the first time on this day. Still smaller tots, who have never even crawled, are said to try to follow, thus creeping for the first time on Ekung's day.

"The people think that this ceremony brings 'plenty piccans' to the town, and, indeed, if you watch the 'play,' so sweet and gay it is, that you cannot but believe it may draw down some such blessing."

Possibly the soft curves of native babies, and the strength of their dimpled limbs, are due to the fact that they are not weaned before they are two years old; sometimes even, like the ancient Egyptians, as we learn from the "Maxims of Ani," they are suckled until the age of three.

When about four years old little maids of the tribe are given a curious ornament called "Nyawhawraw." This is made of twisted brass dangles, looped at the upper end, and ending in a small ball of metal. It is worn from the ceinture in front, and looks much like a row of very elongated little bells, which clash together with a musical tinkle at every movement of the wearer. We were anxious to buy a set of these, and, as they were not exposed for sale in the marketplace, asked a friend if he knew where they were to be procured. His efforts to secure some proved useless, and after awhile it was explained that it is forbidden by the "Woman's Law" to sell Nyawhawraw to any man, lest his possession, however temporary, should affect these in a way which would be felt by the subsequent wearer. Later, an old woman was induced to purchase a set on our behalf.

The prohibition would seem to have come down from a time when the maidens of the tribe were more carefully guarded than at the present day. It was confided to me by one of my women informants, with the explanation that this also was among the mysteries which must be kept from male knowledge; since, should a man of lowly birth who wished to secure for himself alliance with the family of some powerful chief learn the secret, he would only have to single out an infant bride from among the daughters of such a house, and after having secured a set of Nyawhawraw perform certain rites over them and rub them with a particular kind of "medicine." Afterwards he must bribe a woman of the household to see that they were worn by the little maid, and from that time forward it would be impossible for any other man to gain her love.

These little brass ornaments were, until a few years ago, worn up to about the age of ten, when the first real article of dress, namely a narrow sash, was usually given. A few years later an over garment was added. Of late the Efiks, and those Ibibios who have been brought most in touch with civilisation, have begun to give their children garments of European manufacture at a much earlier age.

The Ekung "play" already described, and those which are usually regarded as preparatory to it, and which small boys and maidens "practise" before they are allowed to join the more important society, would seem originally to have been given in honour of the spirits of vegetation. The "Image" of Ekung himself always wears a fringe of palm leaf or long grasses round his loins; while for the lesser festivals the youthful performers must dress themselves in palm or plantain leaves.

The story of such a play was once told me by an Eket woman. It has certain points of interest, as illustrating the life of an Ibibio girl, so is given in full. It is called "Plaintain Leaf":

"Once a woman went to market, but before setting forth she told her daughter to sweep out all the compound during her absence, to fill the jars with fresh water and to prepare coco-yams and other food in readiness for the evening meal. The girl said, 'All that you bid me I will do,' and at once set about the work.

"Not long afterwards two other girls came to the house and said:

"'We have heard that there is to be a fine play to-day in a town on the far side of the river. Come with us to see it.' But the good daughter answered, 'No. My mother bade me fetch water and food and clean all the house during her absence. Were I to come with you, I should not be able to do as she told me.'

"To this the two others replied, 'We will help you with the work, so that all may be finished before we go.' So the girl said, 'If you will first help me, then I will gladly come.'

"On this, all set to work. The visitors began to cook coco-yams and said, 'They are done,' when they were not done. Also they said, 'We have finished cleaning the yard,' when only a little piece had been swept; and, while the good daughter went to and fro fetching fresh water from the spring, they filled up the other jars with rainwater from old pots, which had been standing about for two or three weeks and was no longer pure. On their companion's return they said:

"'We have worked so hard that all is now finished. Let us therefore go.'

"The good girl asked, 'What should one wear for this play?' And the others answered:

"'It is a very special play for which every one must wear plantain leaves.' So they went out and cut these, then fastened them together skirt-wise round their waists, and so set forth gaily.

"Now when they had gone a long way, and the two visitors knew that there would be no time for the good daughter to return and fetch other garments, they ran into the bush and brought out the little waist strips that young girls used to wear, and also dresses to be worn over these--all from the hiding-place where they had concealed them in readiness some time before.

"The good girl said:

"'You told me that we were only going to wear plantain leaves. Now you are robing yourselves in fine garments!' At this they only laughed and answered nothing. The girl continued: 'My mother's house is too far-off. I cannot go back now to fetch other clothes. As I am, I must go with you to see this play.'

"Not long after they had crossed to the other side of the river, they saw a man cutting mimbo high up in a palm tree. For some time he gazed at them and then called down, 'Of these three girls, the one who only wears plantain leaves is more charming than both the others.' When the two gaily dressed maidens heard this they were filled with envy, and said:

"'Give us the plantain leaves to wear, and we will give you our clothes in exchange.' The Plantain Girl answered, 'Very well.' So she took their dresses and gave them her leaves instead. After they had changed they went on once more until they saw another man coming towards them on the road. As he passed he looked back and said to himself, but so that they could hear him:

"'Of these three girls, the one who wears a proper dress is far prettier than the two with plantain leaves.'

"On hearing this the others went aside and consulted with one another saying, 'I thought it was only the leaves which made her more admired than us, but, although we have changed, she is still preferred above us. What can we do therefore? At length one of them said, 'We must change again,' and they did so.

"When they reached the place where the people were playing, the three stood and looked on. When the first dance was over all the finest young men in the town came and crowded round the girl of the plantain leaves, asking her to come to their houses and eat and drink with them. The other two were left quite alone and unnoticed, since no one cared to invite them. Plantain Girl, however, said, 'Let us all go together, otherwise I will stay here with you.' So they went, and when they were seated a cup of mimbo was brought to the beautiful visitor. She drank some, then passed the bowl to her two companions, but they refused it.

"On seeing this, Plantain Girl was much astonished, and said:

"'You two brought me to see the play. Now the people here offer drink to me, and I wish to share it with you, yet you refuse. What is the matter?'

"They answered, 'Nothing'; but after awhile one stood up and whispered to the other, 'Come outside, I wish to speak to you.' So they went into a far-off corner and spoke together. Then they came back and said to Plantain Girl:

"'We are going away for a few minutes. When we are ready to go back home we will come for you and all return together.'

"Plantain Girl smiled, and said, 'Very well,' for she believed them, knowing no guile; but at once these false companions set out for home, leaving her there alone.

"On their way back the two girls came to a stream across the road which all had passed together earlier in the day. It was a juju water, and on the brink they bent down with hearts full of envy and hatred of the companion whom they had deserted, and lifting up their hands called upon the name of the juju and said:

"'We bade this girl wear plantain leaves that we might outshine her, yet all the people prefer her before us. When, therefore, she comes back and stretches out her foot to cross your stream, do not fail to seize her, so that we may be avenged.'

"Plantain Girl waited for her companions to return as they had promised, but when she saw that night was coming on, she could tarry no longer, but said to her new friends 'The other two must have forgotten me and gone home.' So she left the place and set forth alone.

"When she came to the small water which, on her way to the play had hardly reached ankle high, she thought that it would be the same now, so, though darkness had fallen, she stepped bravely in, thinking to cross safely. No sooner had she left the bank, however, than the water rose and rose till it overflowed her head, because of the cruel spell which had been wrought by those two envious ones, when they called upon the juju and begged it to seize her. For three long days she was kept a prisoner beneath the water. Then the same man who had seen her going to the play and was again cutting mimbo near the place, heard her voice crying very pitifully from out the stream. The juju would not let her go free, because of the cruel prayer that had been made. Only sometimes he raised her up to the surface, by the side near the bank, that she might look out for a moment, and see the green trees and the white sky again.

The mimbo man heard her weep and cry:

'I was in the house of my mother, happily working, when two wicked girls called me to go with them and see a play in a far-off town. I asked what dress they would wear, and they said, "Only plantain leaves." So I put on these at their bidding. When we reached the place where the play was held, the people invited me to go and drink. I asked the girls to go with me and offered them part of my mimbo cup, but they refused. There they left me, saying that they would come and fetch me when they were ready to go home. Long I waited, but they never came, so at length I set out alone on my homeward way. The small water rose and covered my head. Since then it has kept me fast held. When the water is full it raises me up so that I can gaze once more upon the white sky, but it will not let me get free, though I try my best both by day and by night.'

When the mimbo man heard this, he came down from the tree and ran as fast as he could, till he came to the house of the girl's mother, and told her all that he had learned. At once the woman went round the town begging those who were strong swimmers to go with her down to the juju water and save her child. All of them tried to do this, but though they dived and swam their hardest none could free the girl, because the juju held her beyond their reach. At length they came back quite exhausted and told the mother, 'It is of no use. We have tried our best, but cannot save your daughter.' On this the woman wept more bitterly than before, while the girl's voice was heard crying from out the stream.

"Now in that town there was an old wife whose body was so diseased that her feet were nearly eaten away. So feeble was she that she could only creep along by means of the bent stick which women sometimes use as a staff."

(It may be not without interest to mention that these staves are made from the flat curved roots of the mangrove tree. The bark is stripped from them, and they are then pointed and shar-pened along the edge, after which they are used for drying fish, being placed in long rows across a rack over the fire with the fish strung upon them. When they have served this purpose, and the dried fish has been sold, the pointed ends are cut off, and they are used as walking-sticks. According to all accounts these form no mean weapon of offence. In shape they are much like the wooden throwing weapons of the present day Bagirimi of Central Africa, or those occasionally found in the sand of the desert, or dug up now and again from ancient Egyptian tombs. The cutting edge of many of these staves is so hard and sharp as to inflict wounds almost as dangerous as machet strokes. Whether as weapon or staff, they appear to be exclusively feminine possessions; for, save in process of making or while in service for drying fish, we have never seen one in the hands of a man.) To continue the story:

"The sick woman crept up to the girl's mother and said: 'These strong ones have failed, yet by the power of Abassi I think that I may be able to bring your daughter up out of the juju water.'

On this the mother cried out:

"'If you are able to do this I shall be more glad than I can say, and will do all that I can to repay you.' The others, however, said:

"'Do not pay any attention to this feeble woman. We who are strong men have tried our utmost and failed. Do not therefore believe this foolish one.' The mother took no notice of them, and only said to her who had offered to help:

"'Let us go and try as you say.'

"Together they went to the water's edge, and when they reached it the sick woman began to plead:

"'I have suffered for many years, and no one could be induced to take care of me. Now, therefore, I pray you, O juju, send out this girl. Perhaps if I free her by means of my prayer her family will look after me for the rest of my days.'

"The juju heard, and lifted the girl up to the surface of the water so that the sick woman could take hold of her hand and draw her out until she lay high and dry upon the shore. After that, with much rejoicing, all went home together.

"When the house was reached the mother of Plantain Girl asked the sick woman, 'Tell me now, what do you want me to do for you in return for what you have done? The old crone answered:

"'Please keep me here and look after me.' The mother asked, 'Will nothing else content you?' But the woman answered:

"'If you want to do something else instead of this, I will only ask one thing. Kill and bring me seven large baskets full of biting flies.' To this the mother replied, shaking her head, 'I do not believe that anyone could do so much. I think, therefore, I had better keep you, and perhaps I can find medicine to cure your sickness.' So she did according to her promise, fed her and bought medicine for her, tending the sick woman till her life's end."

MAIDENHOOD TO MARRIAGE

THE first great event in the life of an Ibibio girl is her entrance into the "Fatting-house," on the occasion of Mbobi--i.e. "The Coming of Small Breasts."

This so-called "Fatting-house" is a room set apart in the home of the parents for the seclusion of daughters while undergoing the process of fattening up, which among West Coast tribes is thought necessary for their well-being. During this time girls are not allowed to go outside the compound walls save on very special and extremely rare occasions. Theoretically they are not supposed to pass the threshold of the "fatting-room." They do no work, and are fed up and pampered on every side.

Before undergoing this seclusion for the first time, young girls are led down to the edge of some sacred pool or stream or that from which the village drinking water is drawn. A sacrifice is offered to the indwelling naiad, and the following prayer recited over each maid:

"Behold! Here comes your child who is about to enter the Fatting-house. Protect her that no evil thing may have power to harm her while she dwells therein."

There is a beautiful appropriateness in this choice of the spirits of streams and pools as the special guardians of maidenhood. So close, indeed, was the tie that among Efiks, and indeed all Ibibios, as well as amid the Ibenos, a small tribe of Ibo race driven by persecution to leave their homes and settle in the southwestern part of the Eket District, a special day in every week was set apart on which none but pure maids might go down to the springs reserved for the drinking water of the village. This day is called in Efik "Akwa Ederi" or "Greater Sunday," to distinguish it from the lesser holiday called "Ekpiri Ederi." Should wives, or those no longer maids, have failed to provide a sufficient supply for the use of their household on the eve of the festival, they must either persuade some maiden to fetch it for them, or thirst till dawn of the following day.

A story in illustration of this ancient tabu was told us first by Mr. David Ekong, son of the former head priest of the chief Ibeno juju, Ainyena, and native minister of the church established by the Kwa Ibo Undenominational Mission in his native town. He stated that he had heard the tale from a very old man of Ibeno. In it the feminine water sprite, a male tree spirit--for among his people the genii of the great trees are thought to be male--and the leopard guardian of sacred spring and grove, all play their part. It was afterwards told us by an Efik woman, the sole difference being that in her account the tree spirit was feminine. It runs as follows:

"There was once a man who had two wives. The daughter of one of them was very sick, and in tending her the mother, whose name was Adiaha Anaw, forgot to go down to the spring and fetch enough water to last them over the sacred day of Idemm (fresh water). When the child thirsted and begged for a drink, the mother took some water from out a jar provided by her fellow wife, since she had none of her own. When the latter discovered what had been done she was very angry, and ordered the poor woman to go and fetch some with which to repay her; although, by so doing, she knew very well that the law of the juju would be broken. Since there was no other way to provide drink for her child, the poor mother was forced to take her water-jar and go down to the spring on the forbidden day. On the way she passed a place where a great tree stood, and, as she drew near, the spirit of the tree stretched out long branches over the road and blocked it so that she could not pass. In great terror and perplexity she waited a while, and would have gone back home again, but that the need of her child urged her on. Then she made a little song, stating her case before the genius of the tree and entreating help and protection. This was the song that she sang:

"'I know that to-day is the day on which only maids may go to the water;
But yesterday I could fetch me none, because of my small sick daughter.
I begged my friends for even a cup, but none would grant such a thing;
So now, I pray you, open the road, and let me pass to the spring.'

When the tree spirit heard the singing, he swept his branches aside and allowed her to pass on; but, a little farther along, she met a great leopard, who stood before her, blocking up the road, so that her heart again sank with fear. Indeed, so terrified was she this time, that she turned and ran back along the homeward path, but again the thought of her child gave her courage to face the terrible beast. To him also she sang, in a sweet, soft voice, bemoaning her hard case; and he too, moved with pity, let her go by. At last she came to the spring, and there, at its brink, she lifted up her voice and sang a third time, entreating forgiveness for thus breaking the rule of the juju. As she finished, the naiad rose from out the pool and spoke gently to her, bidding her take what water she needed without fear. Before she left, the spirit also gave her rich gifts to bear home to her child. So with these she came back laden.

"The first thing which she did after her return was to give back the water taken from the other woman. When the latter saw the presents which her fellow wife had brought back, so envious was she of the other's good fortune that she determined to go herself to the spring, although she very well knew that this was forbidden.

"As the second woman walked along no obstacle blocked her road. The tree spirit did not reach out so much as a twig to stay her, while the guardian leopard let her pass unhindered. Only as she stood on the brink of the spring and bent down to fill her jar did the water-sprite call upon the stream to rise around her. Over all the place it swirled, ever higher and higher, till it overflowed the lips of the terrified woman. In vain did she strive to free herself, for she was held by a force there was no resisting, and at length sank and was drowned in the spring which she had polluted--not, like her fellow wife, from dire need, but only through greed, because she was envious of the rich gifts bestowed upon the other."

It is on account of the cleansing and fertilising powers ascribed to water that maidens are led down to pool or stream before entering the Fatting-house.

In those families which regard a tree as their special guardian, young girls, before entering upon this period of seclusion, are led down to stand beneath the shadow of the mighty trunk while prayers are offered to induce the indwelling Dryad to look favourably upon this "child of the tree" and shed upon her the blessing of strength and fruitfulness, that she may grow up strong and tall, fair to the eye and fitted for motherhood.

As among the Ekoi of the Oban District, so in almost every Ibibio town of any age, there stands a gnarled specimen of Dolichan-drone. This was brought as a young sapling and planted when first the town was founded, and ever since its great mauve-pink flowers have showered their fragrant beauty upon generation after generation of sturdy piccans, slender maids, round-limbed young mothers, and aged crones, who have come to pray beneath its shadow. It is called "The Mother of the Town" (i.e. the largest flower).

One of the best examples of such a tree is to be found at Ikotobo, in the midst of the town playground. So old it is, that the trunk is little more than a shell, though still bearing aloft brave branches of dark waving leaves, and great tufts of blossoms of a tint only to be described by the line in which Dante depicts the apple blooms of his own land:

"Less than of rose and more than violet."

From the gnarled branches of this ancient tree hang great trails of creamy white orchids, the fragrance of which lay like a benediction on the early morning air as we passed by. Within the hollow trunk stood native pots, filled with offerings; for this tree is the "Mother of the Town," and to it come wives, young and old, to pray that "plenty piccans" may be sent to bless their hearths. Hither, too, come ancient women to beg a like boon for their children and grandchildren. Should lightning shiver the aged trunk or tornado strike it down, loud would be the wailing of those who have grown up beneath its shadow.

In most Okkobbor towns stands a great tree, named "Ebiri-bong," to which offerings are made twice a year--at the planting of new farms, and during the yam harvest. This is done with the special purpose of drawing down the blessing of fertility upon the women of the place, as also upon farm and byre.

That something of the beauty of the nature symbols which they worship enters into the character of the race, however dimly felt or understood, is shown, I venture to think, by many an unexpected trait, and more especially by the touching gratitude evinced by some of the women, as well as by the humbler members of the community generally, at my husband's efforts to soften, as far as may be, the hardness of their lot and give practical proof that British justice is indeed no respecter of persons. Time after time attempts made upon his life in revenge for the discovery and punishment of evil practices were frustrated by warnings given, at the peril of their own lives, by such humble members of the race. It would be more than ungrateful, too, not to mention here the loyalty shown by some of the principal Oron chiefs, two of whom publicly risked their lives to save ours.

Such actions are beyond praise--especially when one takes into account the underlying antagonism to white rule ever present among peoples where witch-doctor and fetish priest are untiring in their efforts to stem the power of the white man, and prevent the suppression of those hideous rites which still obtain in little-known parts of the earth such as these.

In this part of the world it is easy, for those to whom the secret has been confided, to know how many maidens are undergoing the fattening Process, for, at the entrance to each town, before the market-place, bundles of little frames--such as are used for the carriage of fresh or dried fish--may be found tied together. Each bundle has been placed there by the family of a girl who is just entering the Fatting-house as an intimation to prospective wooers of the number of brides preparing in the town.

Among the Efiks, and those Ibibios rich enough to bear the expense, free-born girls of good family go twice, and sometimes even thrice, into the Fatting-house before the full marriage ceremony is performed. As already mentioned, the first occasion is called Mbobi, "The Coming of Small Breasts." This usually lasts for three months, during which time the girl undergoes circumcision.

We chanced to be at Adut Nsitt, a town on the upper reaches of the Ubium River, about the time when the daughters of the principal inhabitants were ready to leave the Fatting-house after undergoing this first period of seclusion. One of the chiefs stated that the girls were not due to emerge till a few days later, but that they did so in honour of our presence in the town. Some half-dozen of them came to visit us--the most charming of whom, a small mite of eight summers, unfortunately could not be persuaded to face the perils of the camera.

All wore massive bangles and bracelets of beaten brass or copper, and from a cord round the neck of each dangled a live white chicken, feebly fluttering against the bare brown breast of its bearer. It may be noticed that in the Efik ceremony on the death of a great chief, each of the women is said to wear a similar decoration. [20]

The round brown limbs were painted over with elaborate patterns, in black pigment, made either from the fruit of one of the many Randias which abound in this district, or from the rhizome of the little wild hyacinth-like Ibiri Nsi, to be found in great quantities all over the neighbouring district of Oban.

The second time spent in the Fatting-house is the period in the lives of Ibibio women during which they may be looked upon as most indulged--and, indeed, spoiled to the top of their bent. This second seclusion is fixed at the point where "brook and river meet." For a period varying, according to the wealth of the family, from a few weeks to two years, girls of good position, and even those not "free born" who are looked upon as likely to repay the expenditure--by means of dowry money--are sent once more into the Fatting-house. During this time they again do no work, but are kept in one room, and fed up and pampered in every way. The result is that they emerge, to the admiration of their adoring relatives, and of the townsfolk at large, perfect mountains of flesh--naked, in most parts of the district, save for a few strings of beads and bells, or else decked out with an extravagant array of native ornaments, but always with an air at once arrogant and querulous.

A day is set apart for the first appearance of the girls of each town who are ready to emerge from the Fatting-house. On several occasions we have been present when these swollen specimens of femininity strutted through the market-place enjoying their brief hour of importance; while the men, who at every other period of a woman's existence are looked upon as of superior race, draw back admiringly, to give them passage.

On such occasions the whole charm of these women has temporarily disappeared--at least in the eyes of white people. Of the kindly, gentle air and friendly greeting to be found at all other times, there is no trace in this their little hour of triumph. Only an overweening vanity and bloated self-importance are now manifested.

The wooers, who stand during this parade praising the merits, and value, of the various débutantes, afterwards hurry to the parents with offers of dowry. A marriage is speedily arranged for each, and the young bride quickly finds her place amid the new surroundings; no longer petted, spoiled and pampered--the centre of attention, for whom her family stint and deny themselves--but, only too often, the slighted, hard-worked drudge of her new lord.

Among most Ibibio tribes all such rites are undergone in order to draw down the blessing of Eka Mbopo, the "Mother of the Fatting-house." Among Efiks, however, this is not the case. The second occasion on which a girl of the last-named tribe enters the Fatting-house is called "Abiana Abiana Nkuawhaw," "The Coming of the Full Breasts." The ceremony is also in preparation for marriage, and, should the girl be already betrothed, as is mostly the case, the bridegroom must now pay the first instalment of dowry, or bride price, called "Nkpaw Nkuawhaw Eyen Owon," i.e. "Small Gifts of Fatting."

About Christmastide an Efik bride usually sallies forth to visit her future husband and all his family. There is said to be a special significance in the time chosen for thus emerging from seclusion. It is just before the planting of new farms, and it is thought that the ceremonies proper to the season, which are offered with the object of drawing down the blessing of fertility upon the new crops, will not be without favourable influence upon the maiden who, in this case, stands with anything but "'reluctant feet,' where the brook and river meet." The great ambition of such a one is to become a mother at the earliest possible moment. As one of the tribe naively expressed it: "Young girls just out of the Fatting-house are always looking round the corner, eager to see their first babe."

Indeed, the ceremonies carried out throughout the Ibibio country in honour of Abassi Isua, the God of the Year, with the object of inducing the granting of plentiful crops, are so like those resorted to by the Ekoi to ensure fruitfulness in a wife, that the two ideas would seem to be closely connected.

After a short visit to the bridegroom's household the future bride goes back, loaded with gifts, to live in the house of her mother as before. Should the head wife of the prospective husband belong to a great family, rich and powerful, and should she be sufficiently kindly disposed toward the new bride as to invite the latter to stay with her, the invitation may be accepted for two or three days. Among the gifts borne back to the parents' house on return should always be a thousand wires--in value about one pound sterling--given, to use the Efik expression, "To wash juju." This is sent as a sign on the bridegroom's part of his recognition of the marriage tie.

After this visit rich Efik girls often go back to the Fatting-house, sometimes for as long as two years. During this time they never come out at all, but only walk round within the compound walls.

Should the parents notice that the girl is growing so fat as to endanger her health--to quote the words of my native informant--"they slack off with the 'chop,' and afterwards increase the quantity again."

Just before a daughter leaves the Fatting-house, after this third seclusion, the father and bridegroom consult together and fix upon a date, saying:

"We will hold Etuak Ndum (i.e. 'Chalk Ceremony') on such and such a day."

On the date chosen the girl is dressed out in her best, though the robing may seem rather scanty to European eyes, and sits in state in the midst of one of the inner courts of the compound. "Thither great gifts are borne, sometimes as much as one to two hundred pounds in cash, with string upon string of the finest beads, great bars of coral threaded together, and the costliest of native ornaments. Next the bridegroom enters followed by a long stream of servants bearing 'dashes,' which are laid before the bride. Not for herself alone must such be provided, but for every member of the family down to the little maids, who sometimes get a penny only.

"Several moons earlier a fine house has been prepared in the husband's compound. A 'play' is given, and the bride is borne thither, the performers following. Friends and acquaintances stay until midnight, then at the coming of darkness leave her alone with her husband. Only the bride's mother lingers yet a little, trying to make friends with one of the 'big women' of the compound, begging the latter to instruct the new wife in her duty to her husband and in all native customs, teaching her everything that may pleasure their common lord.

"After a good girl has thus been married she will never leave the compound without her husband's permission. Woman friends may enter to visit her, but no man does so save the male servants sent to clean the rooms or sweep courts."

According to Ibibio ideas the actual marriage tie is entered upon after the payment by the groom to the bride's parents of the major portion of the so-called "dowry money." The first instalment of this constitutes betrothal, and is often paid when the little maid is still very young.

Infant betrothal and marriage are not uncommon. In the latter case the baby bride usually lives with her husband's family; but, save in very rare instances, her youth is respected by him. Should the contrary be proved against a man his conduct is regarded as reprehensible, and the girl's family can claim her back without returning the dowry.

In many cases child betrothal and marriage inflict undoubted hardships upon the unfortunate bride, who thus has no word to say as to her own fate. At the present day many such youthful spouses, on reaching years of discretion, claim the protection of Government to free them from an arrangement in which they had no choice.

A typical case is recorded from Ndun Ukaw town, where a girl, Nko by name, had been betrothed as a very small child. On the day after she came out of the Fatting-house her father said to her:

"The time has now come to carry out the marriage which I arranged for you long ago. Prepare, therefore, to go to the home of the husband to whom I have given you."

The girl pleaded that she did not like the man, and earnestly begged that she might not be forced to wed him; but the father answered:

"This is the one whom I have chosen for you. I will not allow you to refuse. Him you shall marry, and no other."

To which she replied, "Sooner than wed such a one I would rather die."

On hearing this, the father shouted in great anger, "If you do not accept the man whom I have chosen for you, I wish that you may die."

The daughter replied, very gently and with sad dignity, "I have nothing more to say. By your order, sir, I die."

With that she went quietly out, and next morning was found lying dead by her own hand.

The hardships to which unmarried girls among the Ibibios are sometimes subjected may be illustrated by another case, which was brought up before my husband on his first visit to the Native Court at Awa. On this occasion a young girl, daughter of one of the head chiefs of the town, claimed the Commissioner's protection against her father.

It appeared that two suitors were asking her hand, each of whom was in a position to pay the usual "bride price" or dowry of thirty goats. She herself seemed to have set her affections on a third wooer, whom, from some cause or other, her father did not favour. When, therefore, the latter ordered her to take as husband the man whom he had chosen, she refused, and pleaded that if she might not be given to the man of her choice she should at least not be forced into marriage against her will.

In answer, the chief seized her and said:

"If it were not that this bad Commissioner is always going up and down in his district, appearing at all times when and where he is least wanted, I would kill you at once with my own hands for daring to disobey me"

Perhaps it should be remarked that the adjective "bad" has a secondary meaning of "strong," but in this case the circumstances forbid us to hope that the word might have been intended in the more complimentary sense.

The unnatural father bound the girl and thrust her toward the two suitors whom he favoured, saying:

"Take this woman and do to her whatsoever you may choose, that thus she may learn the penalty for having disobeyed me by refusing the man whom I had chosen for her husband."

Delivered over in this way to the mercy of men furious at her rejection of their suit, the wretched girl was dragged along the road to a waste place in the bush. There she was stripped of every garment, and with arms lashed behind forced to endure indescribable outrage. By a fortunate chance, before the last extremity had been reached, a court messenger happened to appear upon the scene. These men are natives employed by Government to serve summonses, make arrests, and generally assist in the carrying out of law and order. This particular one showed considerable courage, for, when drawn to the spot by the girl's cries, he not only ordered the men to desist from their ill-treatment of her, but arrested them when, on the plea that they were justified by the father's permission, in all that they had done, they refused to set the girl free.

The court messenger took them, with the girl, before the chief, and asked whether it was true that the latter had intended the men so to maltreat his daughter. On which the cruel father is reported to have said:

"You cannot touch these men. All that they have done was by my authority. May not a father now do as he chooses with a disobedient child?"

When the case was tried in court the advisory council of chiefs agreed that all had been done as stated, and that they were willing, as a concession to white prejudice in such matters, that some punishment should be inflicted upon the two men. When it came, however, to the question of penalising the chief himself, they pleaded, with a mixture of astonishment and indignation, that a father surely had the right to do as he would with his child, and must, therefore, on no account be punished! Later, when it was explained that whatever might have been native custom in such matters, these abuses could not be tolerated under white rule, the spokesman pleaded again and again--long after his request had been declared impossible--first, that an infinitesimal fine, and afterwards a slowly increasing sum, might be inflicted; but no imprisonment.

Another case, brought up before the Native Court at Oyubia in August, 1913, casts further light on Ibibio ideas of marriage.

A man had lately died, and two people came forward to claim his property, the value of which was computed at about £150. The first of these, Ensinini by name, demanded the whole sum plus the five wives, on the ground that the dead man had not been free born, but was a "member" of the family of which he himself was the head. The second claimant was chief wife of the deceased, and asserted that her late husband had been free born. Since, singularly enough, neither son nor brother of the dead man existed, she demanded that, in default of nearer kin, the goods should come to her. The second wife gave corroborative testimony to the statement that their common husband had been of free birth, and the third was called as a further witness on the matter. In answer a small girl of some eight years appeared. Afterwards the Commissioner asked to see the other two, and a little later a diminutive person of not more than five summers walked shyly up. The chief wife begged to be excused from producing the fifth on the ground that the latter was only just able to walk, and had been presented by herself, after her own payment of dowry, to her late husband only a few weeks before his death.

By native law the whole question turned upon the point as to whether the deceased was free born, or a "member" of the first claimant's family. An equal number of witnesses came forward to swear to positive knowledge as to the truth of each conflicting statement. In the end the bewildered "assessors" suggested that the property should be divided into two equal portions--

one for the male claimant and the other to be distributed between the five wives.

Both sides vehemently objected to such an arrangement, the woman adding, "Why, at any rate, should the other four have a share?" The judgment was, however, upheld by unanimous opinion of the Court, and a long and difficult case seemed at an end, when a chief of great weight rose to propound a question which to native ideas was of first importance, but which, in all probability, would never have struck the white man who was acting as judge.

"To whom," queried the chief, "will the dowry of the five wives be paid on their re-marriage?"

At first sight, to twentieth-century eyes, this question seemed so simple of solution that the Commissioner answered, "Why not to the parents as usual?"

One of the jurors rose, horror visibly struggling with respect, to ejaculate, "Why should the father enjoy a double dowry? Were such a thing allowed the husband's family would lose from both sides!"

By native law in such a case one of two courses was open to the "widows." Either to remain in the family, "bearing children to the dead man's name," as was also decreed by old Jewish custom, or to pay back the dowry, and be free to leave their late husband's family and marry any man whom they might choose.

Although in the case above cited, a member of the Court rose to expostulate against the idea that a father should be allowed to "enjoy" double dowry on account of the same daughter, yet instances axe not unknown in which parents have so arranged matters that the marriage affairs of an only child provided them with a veritable gold mine.

Such was the case of Ama Awsawdi of Okuko, who, so soon as his daughter had left the Fatting-house, gave her in marriage to Obio Esio of Ubodo, receiving as dowry thirty "articles" and one cow-valued together at about £25. A short time afterwards this unprincipled parent inveigled the girl away. The two went on a journey, in the course of which the father arranged a second wedding with one Ukpon Uwe. From this new son-in-law he received eighty articles and one cow, the total value of which was about £50. After a few days, Ama coaxed the girl to leave her second husband and go away with himself to Calabar. She was undoubtedly attractive, and the father considered that a few shillings laid out on a gown and bead ornaments for her were likely to prove a good investment. For considerably less than one pound sterling he succeeded in attiring the girl so sumptuously that a well-known citizen named Asukwaw Etin was induced to offer a hundred articles and one cow, i.e. about £60, as bride price. Since this third son-in-law was a man of greater weight and position than the others of whom he had so easily rid himself, Ama probably thought it necessary to be a little more careful in his dealings on this occasion. He therefore went to consult one or two friends as to the next step in his career of crime.

"I am thinking of taking away my daughter to a far country," he said, "and there hiding her until I can arrange a fresh marriage. I do not want anyone to know that I am running away with the girl, lest she should be pursued and brought back; so please help me to hide our tracks."

The men consulted were too conservative to receive such revolutionary ideas with favour. They therefore protested against the plan, but Ama replied:

"I know what I am doing, and would not act thus in defiance of custom without pressing cause; but my debts are really too heavy, and I can see no other way of paying them! That is my reason for wanting to run away with the girl."

Since the friends on whose help he had counted would have none of his plan, Ama shrugged his shoulders and, being an energetic soul, proceeded to carry it out by himself. The daughter was abducted and concealed in what the father thought a safe retreat. Matters were progressing most favourably in the direction of her fourth nuptials when a cruel fate intervened with the news that the three defrauded husbands had joined forces and were on the way to demand a return of their dowries. Such a contingency was unforeseen and unprovided for. The excellent parti with whom the new alliance had been all but arranged, at a higher rate than ever before, had to be abandoned, and the pair disappeared in the direction of Mbukpo, where they were lost sight of, but are still in all probability, pursuing their profitable career amid "fresh woods and pastures new."

Viewed in the light of a provider of dowries, the story of the mother who, when faced by the necessity of giving up one of her children, chose to keep the daughter rather than the son on account of the high bride price promised by the former, becomes quite comprehensible.

WEDDED LIFE AND MOTHERHOOD

PROBABLY most white men on first coming to Africa are inclined to look upon black women as prone to suffer beneath the oppression of their men folk.

It was with much this idea that my husband went to the Oban District, and the glee of its sturdy amazons, who had long ago reduced the male Ekoi to a state of becoming humility, on recognising this attitude on the part of the first Commissioner sent them by Government, can be better imagined than described! No one is quicker than these "unsophisticated" peoples to recognise any such bias, and the consequent pose adopted by the militant wives was pathetic in the extreme, and the more convincing in that their meek male folk hardly ventured upon a word of defence. When the "hideous cruelty" of which one wife complained was, however, found to consist in her husband's refusal to marry any other woman save herself, so that no secondary wife was available to help in the house-work, and the tyranny of a father over his daughter, a child of eight, was discovered only to have been shown in making use, without her permission, of a cooking-pot which he had himself given her some time before, the Commissioner's point of view naturally changed somewhat.

Taught by such experience, we arrived in the Eket District with an open mind as to the relation of the sexes; but this philosophic attitude was to be rudely dispelled. The land of the Ibibios may be taken as typical of those where fetish and witch doctor reign supreme, and where woman is looked upon as a mere chattel of father or husband.

Left to themselves, the Ibibios may perhaps be considered, along certain lines, as a moral people; although the old idea, which lingered in mid-Europe until comparatively recent times, that a host should place all in his house, even to the honour of his wife, at the disposal of a guest, yet obtains here. To quote the naive statement of my informant:

"When a friend comes to visit him the husband will often go out of the house, leaving the new-comer alone with his wife, so as to give them a chance. . . . Afterwards the two men drink together in token of friendliness, and to show that no claim for compensation will be made by the husband."

In the old days crimes of unfaithfulness would appear to have been far more uncommon than at present, probably owing to the terrible penalties inflicted. At times the death of both guilty parties was exacted; while, as a comparatively mild punishment, the lover was often forced to sell himself into slavery in order to raise sufficient money to meet the heavy fine imposed.

The chiefs expressed themselves as unanimous in wishing the penalties for infidelity to be made more severe than the comparatively light damages exacted at present; but their attitude is very one-sided. All of them desire that, as in the old days, no woman should be allowed to claim divorce save on the grounds of grave ill-treatment, while many wish for the still older rule to be enforced, that it should not be allowed to women for any cause whatever. As one of them explained:

"Should a man beat his wife very cruelly she can always run away to her father, who will give her good advice, such as: 'Obey your husband in everything, and always strive to please him. Make his will yours; then you will no longer be ill-treated.'"

That many husbands still regard their wives as mere chattels is proved by case after case, of which the following, brought before my husband in the Native Court at Eket only a short time ago, may serve as typical:

Offong Udo Akpa Imo thought that he had reason to suspect his wife Unwa of infidelity. In order to induce her to confess to this he tied her hands to two stakes firmly driven into the ground and so far apart that she lay with arms extended as if crucified. He then proceeded to torture her by forcing native pepper into her eyes and in other ways, which, though recounted in Court as mere matters of everyday occurrence, are such as it is impossible to describe. Yet the man only acted within the rights given him by the law and custom of his tribe.

According to some accounts, it would appear that the usual torture inflicted under such circumstances was, after stripping and binding the woman in the way just described, to cover her with thousands of the fierce black ants which abound in the bush, and which the husband had previously collected for the purpose.

Such cases are not confined to the Ekets, but might be repeated ad nauseam in connection with every tribe in the district. The Orons, as nearest to Calabar, and therefore most in touch with civilisation, should show some advance in the treatment of their women, yet the following case brought before the Native Court in August, 1913, is quite typical. During the course of the evidence Eyo Okon Mbukpa, stated on oath:

"Mbit Ese Ewan was my husband, but I wish to be divorced from him. Last year he wounded me, but afterwards took a lot of trouble to cure my wound. Later he asked me to come back. At first I refused, to do so, but afterwards agreed. Through his roughness he broke one of my bones, on account of which, when my child was born, I nearly died. For two months afterwards I could hardly walk. A third time he came, but I refused him. On that he knocked me down and dragged me, naked, before the townsfolk. . . . Next morning he flogged me very cruelly."

There was no question by the husband.

Ating, a fellow townsman, stated on oath:

"I am no relation of Eyo Okon's, neither am I her 'friend.' I saw Mbit Ese come to her. He stripped her, lifted her feet in the air and beat her head upon the ground, then dragged her along it. The girl kept shouting to me, so at last I went to her help. My cousin's wife told me that the bone was broken, and Eyo was very clever to have got her child safely born."

Mbit Ese Awan, the husband, sworn, stated:

"I did not hold her feet in the air nor beat her head upon the ground. I only dragged her along it."

There were, however, too many witnesses against him, and the charge was proven in all respects.

While many women have taken advantage of the protection afforded by white rule to break away from the old stern code as to marital fidelity, many are still faithful to their husbands, as has been proved by no inconsiderable number who have resisted to the last extremity outrages sought to be forced upon them. Not only this, but that a distinct desire for monogamy does exist among Ibibio women is shown by the frequency of cases in which wives have 'administered love philtres to their husbands in the hope of thus capturing the whole affection of their dusky lords. This will be more fully treated of later, in the section devoted to magic.

In those few cases when a much-married man of the tribe has been denied the blessing of children, the "medicine doctor" consulted as to the cause of the misfortune has been known to advise the putting away of all wives save one. The following story, illustrating such a case, was told me by one of my women informants--a Christian convert--as a proof of the advantage of monogamy over polygamy. In all save names, it bears a striking resemblance to a tale recounted by Mr. Elphinstone Dayrell in his collection of "Ikom Folk Stories." [21]

"Once a very great chief named Ekpenyong Abassi dwelt among us. He was so rich that his house was filled with treasures. His flocks and herds multiplied beyond those of other men. His palm groves produced their golden clusters in such numbers that the gatherers grew weary of cutting, and when he sent out his slaves to fish in the rivers they brought back catches so heavy that they staggered beneath the weight.

"While still young, Ekpenyong married many wives; but in spite of his great wealth he was not happy, for no babe was sent to bless his hearth. His days were therefore spent in sadness, lest he should die without a son to bury him with due honour and pour libations to his ghost.

"To and fro in the land went the chief from one famous juju man to another, seeking a 'medicine' which might take away his curse and cause a child to be born. To each he gave great gifts, but no matter what was paid for charm or magic rites, all proved of no avail. At length word came of a medicine man, said to be very strong in the knowledge of secret things, who had come down from the Kameruns, where much magic dwells, and was now staying in a part of the district far away from the home of Ekpenyong.

"No sooner had the chief heard of the fame of this stranger than he set forth, taking with him a great 'dash' of wires and cloth. Spears, too, he took and cattle, with other fine things borne by a train of slaves. When he reached the house of the juju man he told the latter all his trouble, and asked what he must do in order that a son might be granted him.

"The priest consulted his oracle and at length announced:

"'All your wives you must put away from you save one only, Adiaha by name. Then you must raze to the ground the houses in which the other women used to dwell. Press down and smooth the earth over the place till none may see that dwellings once stood there. Then build a quite new home for Adiaha and offer in sacrifice before it a white goat, a white fowl and many eggs. From the door-lintel of the new house, on the inside, let a piece of white cloth be hung. Then go yourself to the riverside, and, casting away the clothes which you have formerly worn, go down into the water, taking care that it laves every part of your body and flows even above the crown of your head. After this, dress yourself from head to foot in new garments and, returning, sleep alone in your house.

"'Meantime, let Adiaha go to the pool where the great juju dwells, and, after likewise casting from her her garments, let her slip into the water until it flows above her head. After which bid her put on a white gown never before worn, so that she should be an entirely fresh woman, and, thus robed, let her go silently into the house prepared for her and there await your coming.'

"On hearing this, Ekpenyong thanked the medicine man, and after leaving his offering went home with new hope in his heart. No sooner did he reach the compound than he sent to call all his wives before him. From farm or cooking-hearth they came trooping forth to welcome him home; but when they heard the news which he brought their joy was turned into wailing. Some pleaded that they should not be driven forth; some reviled Adiaha, and said that it was but the trick of a jealous wife, who had bribed the juju man to give her husband this advice, so that they might all be humbled while she alone reigned in their stead. Adiaha wept bitterly at their hard words, for, indeed, she was fond of many of them and sorry to lose their companion-ship, but she comforted herself at the thought that at length a son was about to be born to her.

"Ekpenyong sent to his farms to fetch yams and plantains in great quantities, and took from out his storehouse chains and anklets, with bracelets and other rich gifts, all of which he gave to the discarded wives; so that they went forth well dowered and could easily find other husbands. When all had left the compound, everything was done according to the advice of the wise juju man. The houses where the old wives had dwelt were pulled down, and the place smoothed over and planted, so that none might see that a dwelling had been there. Then a new home was made for Adiaha, after which husband and wife went down to bathe, and did, to the very least thing, as they had been bidden. Before many moons had passed the woman felt a stirring beneath the breast, and told her husband, whereon they both rejoiced greatly.

"Next day husband and wife went together before the juju which dwelt under the sacred water in which Adiaha had bathed. With them they took a goat as offering, and prayed to the spirit of the pool to watch over the unborn babe. The blood of the victim was then poured over Adiaha's forehead, while Ekpenyong sacrificed white fowls and eggs that she might not suffer greatly when her child should come. [22]

"On the birth of the boy the chief gave a 'play' for all the young men and women of his town, that they also might rejoice in his good fortune. A few months later he got together a great 'dash' and sent it to the wise juju man, thanking him for the advice which had proved of such advantage, and asking that the oracle might be consulted as to whether this child would live, and also how many further children would be granted him. The answer was returned that the first son would certainly thrive, and that twenty-one children in all might be hoped for.

"On learning this good news the chief gave another great feast. Afterwards he summoned all his slaves before him and bade them cut bush and clear the land in readiness for the planting of very large farms, since now he must begin to make provision for so numerous a household.

"In course of time other children were born to the couple, until they were surrounded by a large family of sturdy sons and daughters. Always Chief Ekpenyong guarded Adiaha tenderly and saw that she was well served, for he feared that some of his old wives might be jealous and seek to do her a hurt.

"After many years the twenty-first child arrived, and the chief knew that no more were to follow. So he said to his wife, 'You must be weary from bearing so many babes. Now, therefore, rest, for the juju so wills.'

"Always when the chief went on a journey to a neighbouring town, or even but a small way to visit his farm or make sacrifice in the juju house, all his children accompanied him. In their midst he walked, rich and happy, and many of the townsfolk envied his good fortune.

"Now, in the same town there dwelt a lesser chief whose heart was very sore when he considered the prosperity of Ekpenyong. Long he pondered as to how he might best wreak vengeance upon his prosperous neighbour, and sometimes in crocodile form--for he was full of witchcraft and could send forth his soul in this guise--he used to creep up a little stream which lay near the back of Ekpenyong's compound spying out how he might best injure the man whom he hated. Only he never dared go very near to the house because he feared the juju which was hung therein, since it was very powerful, and he dreaded lest it should kill him on account of his evil witchcraft.

"Now among the 'witch company' to which this man belonged was one of Chief Ekpenyong's former wives. To her, therefore, he opened the matter, asking if she had never heard of a way by which the power of this particular juju might be circumvented. The woman demanded why he wished to know, and he answered that he, together with many of the townsfolk, was weary of seeing the continuous prosperity of Ekpenyong, and therefore wanted to get rid of him and all his family, so that the latter's great possessions might be divided up among them-selves. To this the woman answered that she also was jealous of Adiaha, because the latter had been preferred before her, and also because so many children had been born to this woman, while she herself remained barren. They therefore consulted together and made a plan-------." But that is another story. [23]

In the foregoing story both Ekpenyong and Adiaha were bidden to go down to the water and bathe so that their bodies might be laved from head to foot. This would appear to have been ordered, not only on account of the fertilising powers ascribed to water in this region, but also as a means of breaking the curse of sterility under which both were suffering.

Such an idea seems not unconnected with the ancient Babylonian belief in the power of water as an antidote to evil spells, mentioned by Mr. R. C. Thompson in dealing with charms and magical preparations. He says:

"Of these the simplest was pure water, which was sprinkled over the possessed person at the conclusion of an incantation, and this had a double meaning, symbolising as it did the cleansing of the man from the spell, and the presence of the great God Ea, whose emanation always remained in water and whose aid was invoked by these means."

To a similar belief in the purifying power of water the ancient Roman lustral ceremonies may also be ascribed.

*   *   *   *   *

An Efik woman once expressed her ideas on the advantage of monogamy in quaint, halting English as follows:

"Among our people, if a man gets plenty wives and then goes outside and brings in yet another, the first ones get vexed at this, so trouble comes in that family. Perhaps one wife goes out and finds another man. For this the husband flogs her. She then takes out a summons against him and says, 'I will not stay with that husband any more.' The custom of marrying many wives brings trouble for all women in our country. Women themselves sometimes keep as many as four 'friends,' 'well hidden.' If the husband finds out, he goes bring palaver. Sometimes he flogs the offending men. Sometimes he summonses them. Sometimes a big man has many wives, and one of them wants him to love her past all others. Then she makes medicine and gives him. He says she wants to kill him, and therefore brings her before Court. Some men get wife for house, but no be fit to buy clothes for her. Then another man brings clothes and gives her and the woman takes some of these and 'dashes' to her husband, on which he accepts them and lets her go her own way. At times a husband says he will go walk. Then he goes out, but turns back when out of sight and goes to another place. On his return the wife asks, 'Whence do you come?' He answers, 'I only walk.' Wife says, 'What time did you come back from walk?' He says, 'No ask that. I no be boy.' On which the wife begin to vex. Sometimes a wife is good woman, but no get piccan. Therefore husband says, 'No want you any more.' Some men say, 'If wife goes church will not have her again.' Some women for this part refuse to marry man if he no go church. Say, 'No want to marry you.' To which man reply, 'Very well, no want you--another man can marry you.' Men like to have plenty wives because each can do certain things and then more work is done.

"Sometimes if husband flogs wife she summonses him. Then he goes prison and she goes for another man. When husband comes out of prison he goes kill the woman. Takes the other man's other wife in exchange, and goes to his house. He does not kill the man, because it was the first woman's fault!

"If a man gets plenty money women like to marry him, but when the money finishes wife runs away and says, 'Do not want you now.' To which the man replies, 'Cannot go. You married me, and must stay whether I have money or not.'

"One woman, her husband went for some place to another man's house, because he loved other man's wife. Leopard caught him and killed him. Then wife began to cry. Said, 'If husband had stopped with me he would not have died so.'

* * * * *

Among some Ibibios a custom still obtains through which it is hoped by sympathetic magic to ensure fruitfulness to a bride. When for the first time the new wife enters her husband's house he leaves her so soon as she has crossed the threshold and goes to the compound of some friend to whom a "fine piccan" has been granted. He then hastens back with the babe in his arms, and, entering the bride chamber, says, "Look! This is my piccan." This is done in order that many children may be born to them also.

Again, when the young wife is about to bear her first babe, the husband often goes out and invites other small folk into the house. A meal has been prepared, and while the little guests are busily feasting he calls to his wife, "Just as many piccans are now in our house so may you bear plenty for me, that in time it will be filled with our children!"

A juju of special renown as the protector of women and the bestower of fertility is that called Isemin. Pools sacred to this spirit are to be found in all the country round Awa. One of the most celebrated of these lies near the border of the town of Mkpokk, and thither one early September day we went, about the time of the new yam harvest. Through the town playground we passed, then turned to the right beneath a screen of boughs which had to be held aside for us to enter a path, almost invisible at first, but later showing a track deep-worn by the feet of worshippers, who for centuries had followed this road to the sacred water. Beneath a continuous archway of overhanging boughs we passed, low bending of necessity, under leafage so thick as to produce a soft green twilight, till the edge of the holy pool was reached.

Thither, at the new yam festival, all the women and girls of Mkpokk go in procession at dawn. "Naked as the breeze" they pass to bathe in the stream. All men must keep in the houses during the performance of this rite, and should one be found hiding in the bush during this, one of the most sacred of the feminine mysteries, the old native law condemns him to death. Even now a fine of one goat and a hundred manillas would be exacted by the angry women; while the chances of that man living to see the dawn of another Isemin day would also not be very great, for even the protection of Government would hardly avail to save him from the thousand and one subtle poisons which are still unknown to white men. It is believed that, should male eye gaze upon these women as they go by unveiled to show themselves before Isemin, the object of the rite would be brought to naught, and the blessing of fruitfulness which it is designed to draw down would in consequence be denied to the town.

Later, one of my women informants explained the matter to me more clearly than such things would seem usually to be formulated in the minds of primitive people such as these. She confided the matter with a charm and delicacy of expression hardly to be expected from a woman typical of those of this region.

"As a bride on her wedding night," said the narrator, "yields herself in all ways to the will of her new-made lord, so at harvest time maids and matrons present themselves before the great juju, Isemin, unrobed and awaiting his will, that perchance he may enter within those whom he chooses, thus shedding the blessing of fertility upon our town."

The eldest of the band, low bending, presents a sacrifice of corn and fish, symbolising fertility on earth and beneath the waters.

In every town throughout this part of the district a shrine of this juju may be found, and when a girl marries away from her native place she joins the Isemin of her husband's people.

Great pythons are thought to guard the dwelling-place of the deity--a little hut overlooking the stream. Many snakes, as we can testify from our experience, have their homes near by, and these no man may kill. To the inhabitants of Mkpokk and the neighbouring village of Okat snake flesh is tabu "because snakes are sacred to Isemin," and were this law broken the juju would avenge himself by withholding the blessing of fertility from the town, while a devastating pestilence would fall upon the sacrilegious inhabitants. For these great serpents, set as guardians to the mysteries of Isemin, like the famous snakes of Æsculapius, also bestow health upon the countryside.

Some half-mile off is to be seen the shrine of the juju Okwu Okat, before which girls of the aforementioned place must show themselves on entering the Fatting-house. On this occasion custom ordains that they should wear ornaments made from young palm leaves.

DOMESTIC LIFE

FOR some reason or other Ibibio women seem to be, on the whole, of higher type than the male portion of the community. So marked, indeed, is the difference in appearance that at first sight they might be taken to be of another race from the men. Professor Keith, F.R.S., informs us that this difference is very strongly shown in those skulls submitted to him for examination.

The men are fairly industrious as regards occupations which custom has decreed should fall to their share; such, for instance, as cutting bush for the new season's farms, tending palm trees, and collecting nuts and kernels. They also build the houses, raise the heavier fishing nets, and, as a general rule, paddle the canoes. On the women, however, falls by far the greater proportion of labour. They do the principal part of the farm work, much of the fishing, often undertake the smoking, and always the marketing of the "catch," together with the making and selling of the great water jars and other native pottery.

To give a typical day in the lives of these overworked drudges:

At dawn the wife chosen to share the couch of her lord during the past night rises and brings him water in which to wash. It is in this water, by the way, that she sometimes pours a few drops of the love-potion which she trusts may steal away his affection from the other wives and rivet it upon herself.

Next she goes to the small shrine where stand the row of rude fetishes, often no more than rough sticks driven into the ground, with possibly a slit cut across near the top to represent a mouth. These are the "gods of the week." Before the one which represents the guardian of this particular day she lays an offering, praying that the indwelling spirit will be with her till the morrow's dawn, shielding and prospering her throughout all her undertakings. After this she begins her share of the day's toil, fetching water and firewood, cooking the morning meal and other house or farm work.

Later she loads herself with the palm nuts, oil, yams, cassava, native pots, or other merchandise got ready for the purpose, and sets off either for the native market or the European factory. After a march of anything up to fifteen miles, or even more, she must dispose of her wares and return on her weary tramp, laden sometimes, according to statements made by agents of some of the principal firms on the coast, with a load occasionally as much as sixty pounds in weight, for which she has exchanged her produce. She arrives at home in time to prepare the evening meal for her lord, whom she finds, more often than not, idly awaiting her return amid his gossips in the village "palaver shed."

When it is remembered that in many districts all merchandise is borne by hand, for not even the roughest of carts exists for the conveyance of goods, and that by far the greater proportion of native produce is carried on the heads of women, the opening up and improvement of roads becomes a matter of the greatest importance. On our first visit to the eastern part of the Eket district the main roads were found to be blocked before the entrance to every village, as well as to the more important of the farm plantations, by stockades which stretched right across the thoroughfares. The only means of surmounting these was to climb by two trunk sections set on end and firmly driven into the ground. The lower of these was about one and a half feet, and the second almost double that height. When one stood upon the latter, one had to step over the fence on to a similar block on the other side, and so down--only to be met by a like obstacle at the other end of the town. The difficulty which these stockades added to the task of weary, over-burdened women-traders can be imagined. Happily the roads are now open and so improved that, according to the testimony of merchants at the principal commercial centre of the district, trade has shown a very large increase in consequence.

In spite of the drudgery of their lives many of the women seem bright and kindly, and nearly always have a pleasant smile and word of greeting as one passes them on the road.

To the feminine portion of the community, as has already been mentioned, is owed the one Ibibio fine art--that of pottery. Without a wheel, or any aid save their own hands and a fragment of broken sherd, these women build up, from the blue clay of the locality, richly ornamented bowls and giant jars, which in beauty of line and decoration rival those which we discovered at Abijang and Nchopan on the Cross River, made by Ekoi women potters. In the Duke of Mecklenburg's book, "From the Congo to the Niger and the Nile," the pottery of the Mangbatu is mentioned as far superior to that of any other negro race. I venture to think that this opinion would hardly have been maintained had the surely far more graceful examples to be found among Southern Nigerian tribes been brought to the notice of the distinguished author.

Among Ibibios this talent is given widest play in the creation of new forms for the vases and bowls placed upon burial mounds or within the erections built as memorials to dead chiefs. It is true that no trace of the graceful flying-buttress-like handles and slender necks of the Ekoi water jars has come to our notice here; but the forms of the vessels themselves and the care expended on the raised decorative motifs are surely as fine as any in Africa.

The difference in the Ibibio estimate of the value of life between men and women was poignantly illustrated on one occasion when we were passing along the Oron-Eket road.

Suddenly on rounding a corner not far from the eighth milestone we saw a body lying prone. The feet were upon the grassy border, but the head lay in the full glare of the pitiless sunshine, so near the middle of the path that care was needed in passing on the motor bicycle. As soon as it was possible to stop we went back to give what help we could, and found the body to be that of a youngish woman, but so shrunken by sickness or neglect that the limbs were little more than sticks, while the breasts were like those of an aged crone. She lay face downwards, shaken by shuddering sobs; but though a stream of wayfarers was passing, none took the slightest notice--a fallen log would have excited more, since that would in all probability have been carried away for firewood. We did what we could for the moment, and commandeered two of the passers-by to get the loan of a native bed from a neighbouring compound. On this the little shrunken form was carried back to the sleeping-sickness camp. There, as we well knew, the kindest care awaited her, but alas! it came too late to save this pitiful piece of human jetsam, and she died at dawn.

By a strange coincidence, for never before in our many journeys up and down had we found anyone stricken upon the road, hardly a mile farther we came upon the body of a man apparently felled by sunstroke. He, however, had been carried beneath the cool shade of a wayside clump of bamboo, and the passers-by, both male and female, had set down their loads and were eagerly doing all in their power to restore him.

Many Ibibio women are stunted in growth, while some are positively dwarfs. This is possibly due to the heavy loads which they carry in youth. Once while staying at the rest-house at Ikotobo we noticed a woman turn the corner of the Uyo road. On her head she bore a section of tree trunk at least eight feet in length and two in girth. The late Dr. Foran, who was spending the evening with us, remarked as to the extraordinary weight which these people seem capable of bearing. Not long before he said he had met a man carrying a load of firewood which he computed could hardly have been less than 150 pounds in weight. Since the bearer was not of robust appearance he stopped to caution him as to the risk he was running by so doing, but the old man refused to listen, and passed on. Before his destination was reached he sank to the ground, and subsequent investigations proved that he died from a broken neck caused by the strain of his load. It is comparatively rare, however, for men to undertake such services, the burden of which almost invariably falls upon the women.

A particularly diminutive specimen ran up to us one evening on our arrival at the seashore town of Ibeno. The sunset glow still lingered in the sky, and through the clear air the great peak of the Kamerun Mountain was clearly to be seen; while farther off the islands of Fernando Po and San Thome were silhouetted against the evening light. It is so unusual for the atmospheric condition to make it possible to see these points that my husband sprang ashore and set up the theodolite in all haste that angles might be taken towards the distant heights. These had, for us, associations almost sacred, since they were so closely connected with our friend, the late Boyd Alexander.

When the small dusky figure first approached and stood humbly waiting, we thought that she had only come to bid us welcome, and, as each moment of light was precious, would have dismissed her with the word "Echiro" ("Greeting").

The answer "Echiranda" was, however, given in so faint a voice and with such a sobbing catch of the breath, that we turned to see what was the matter.

It was a pitiful enough sight on which our eyes fell. The woman's right car was all but cut off; while her cheek, throat, and side were cruelly gashed and clotted with blood. All for so small a thing! Merely a quarrel over a few feet of yam patch, which was claimed both by herself and a fellow wife preferred before her in the affection of their common husband.

By rights the following account should be included under the heading of "Juju," but it illustrates so poignantly the estimation in which women are held among this people, that I have chosen rather to give it here. It was told us by Idaw Imuk of Idua Eket.

"In olden days, before Government came to our country, there was a great juju in our town, the name of which was Abo Abom.

"Year by year sacrifices were made before it. First of all the members gathered together in the Egbo House and the chief priest of the cult announced: 'Now is the time for sacrifice.'

"Then, from all the countryside, the people collected yams and fowls and brought them before the juju to induce him to protect them, so that none might die within the year. Then, when the provisions had been stored within the Egbo House and the members were gathered together, the head priest sent forth messengers to seek a man with neither father nor brothers. It did not matter whether or no he had sisters, because, should these come making a fuss and weeping, the members had but to answer, 'Even if we show you your brother's blood, what can you do?'

"When such a man had been led before the meeting, with hands tied behind the back with cords well tested as to strength, his body was rubbed all over with dye from the camwood tree. Next he was placed before the juju and there tightly bound by throat and ankles to a stout stake. No further harm was then done to him; he was just left to die of thirst and starvation.

"After making this offering, the members went forth to that part of the sacred bush where the juju dresses were kept. There they robed themselves, and then came back, clad in full dress, to give their play in the town.

"No woman might see this play, but all were curious, even to the young girls, and talked it over among themselves, saying, 'What is there in these rites which it is forbidden us to see?'

"Now, one woman of the place, Adiaha Agbo by name, thought, 'If I hide myself in the bush, no one will know of it, and then I shall learn this great secret which the men keep from us.'

"So she hid, and spied upon the company as they returned.

"When, however, the juju image passed the place where she lay concealed, he called to his followers in a terrible voice:

"'I see one woman named Adiaha Agbo hiding in the bush, in order that she may learn what it is not lawful for woman to know.'

"On hearing this, Adiaha was so terrified that her limbs failed her, and she could not even attempt to escape.

"The juju called to his followers: 'Go to that spot. Drag forth the woman, and bring her before me.'

"All was done as he said. The juju members surrounded the woman, brandishing their machets and shouting. One cried, 'She must be killed.' But another, who was a kinsman, answered:

"'If you want to kill her, you must first ask permission of her owner.'

"(The woman was free born, but married, and, according to our rule, a husband is the owner and possessor of all his wives.)

"To this the juju answered: 'Since you speak thus impertinently we will first kill the woman, and then see what further should be done in the matter.'

"On this the members began to consult together. Those who wished her to be killed drew on the one side, those who were in favour of asking her husband as to her fate on the other. The first party said:

"'We play this play as our fathers played it hundreds and hundreds of years ago. So far as we know, no woman has ever seen it before. We remember those who have witnessed other jujus without permission and were killed for it. Therefore she also must die.' Whereon they fell upon the woman and slew her on the spot.

"When the other side saw that she was already dead, they said: 'We will no longer belong to this juju. It is wrong to kill a woman without her husband's permission.' On that they fell upon the murderers and slew seven of them; after which they ran and hid themselves in the bush.

"When a little time had passed, the fugitives talked together over all that had happened, and said to one another:

"'Now that we have killed our brothers of the juju, of what use to live any longer? Let us rather slay ourselves also.' To this they agreed, so each man fell upon his machet and died in the bush by himself.

"When the catastrophe was noised abroad, the people of neighbouring towns came to Idua and asked the surviving townsfolk: 'What is the cause of this that we hear? Never did we see such a thing before! If, therefore, you do not pay a fine of one cow to each town all of us will join together and kill the remainder of you; because you Iduans have offended against our rule. If there was a dispute about a woman who had kinsfolk to take her part, you should not have killed her, but have bidden her family ransom her at the price of another who was kinless and about whom, therefore, there would have been no trouble. Had you done so, all the men now dead would have been alive to-day!'

"So Idua was forced to pay a cow to each of the neighbouring towns in order that the palaver might be settled, for the Iduans were not strong enough to withstand all those who had joined together against them."

Ibibios are perhaps unusually bloodthirsty, for crimes of violence were so frequent that for months after our arrival scarcely a day passed without a man or woman running in to claim the protection of the District Commissioner--often with hideous gun or machet wounds to show in plea. Should a day fortunately have gone by without such incident the morrow usually more than restored the average.

One evening just as dusk was falling a woman crept up the steps which lead to the veranda of the station bungalow. Her skin showed that curious grey pallor which intense fear substitutes for the warm brown of the native, and out of her drawn face the dark eyes gleamed, large and terror-filled. Her name, she said, was Unwa of Efa, in the Uyo District. She was now on a visit to a friend at Ikot Atako some few miles off on the far side of the river. To her, hot-foot, had come a brother with the news that Chief Ikombo of Efa had slain their sister Adia Inaw, who was one of his wives, and had afterwards cut off the head and arms of the corpse. According to the testimony of a friend, Amaw Ima by name, Ikombo had "fled to bush" immediately after the murder, and was lying in wait for Unwa herself in order to slay her because she had formerly advised her sister against wedding him.

The reason given for the crime was that the chief had quarrelled with his wife about some small matter, and then charged her with placing poisonous leaves in his food and pipe. Well knowing the danger of such an accusation, the unfortunate woman went before the chiefs of the town and asked what she should do. By their advice she took out a summons against her husband, claiming divorce. His answer was to slay and mutilate the woman who had dared appeal to the protection of the law. Then, knowing himself outcast, he took to the bush, determined to glut himself with vengeance, and trusting that the difficulty of capture might save him from paying the penalty of his crime.

Unwa came in terror of her life to beg protection, for she dared not return to her town so long as this peril was abroad. She appeared grateful for permission to remain until it was possible to arrange with the Commissioner for her safe return. Her story is uninvestigated, and how the matter ended we never learnt, owing to our unexpectedly early departure from the District.

* * * * *

On another occasion when my husband was visiting the Awa Native Court, a woman, splendidly built and with a fine air of courage and resolution unusual among those of her race, stood forth in Court and called to him.

There was a stir among the men present, several of whom busied themselves in persuading her to sit down and keep silence. Among these a lean old man, with one glittering eye-- the other had been closed by a machet stroke--and a most malevolent expression, was particularly prominent. Another case was beginning: plaintiff and defendant were already in the box, so the judge went on, apparently unconscious of the woman, but keeping her in view all the time. Many efforts were made to entice her outside the building; but she resolutely refused to stir, and, at the end of the case in hand, sprang forward again--this time right to the front of the Court. On her hip, encircled by the right arm, sat a sturdy piccan, while the left was flung out towards the Commissioner, and from her lips demands and entreaties poured forth in a flood of excited eloquence.

It transpired that the woman, Nwa Udaw Uko by name, had been put into prison for no fault at all, but merely on demand of the hawk-eyed old chief, named Etesin, who had busied himself in trying to suppress her when she first strove to draw attention to her case. His plea was that "Some white man or other at some time had ordered her piccan to be given up to him so soon as it was able to walk alone; and that, since she refused to do so, he had induced the Native Court clerk to imprison her. He was unable to give the least indication by which the alleged judgment could be traced; she, on the contrary, pleaded that the chief had no authority over her or any of her people, save that he had seized several of them and sold them into slavery, the last occasion being only three years before. Since there were no witnesses on either side, save the woman's husband, who came forward, at her call, to corroborate what she said, the case had to be adjourned; but the woman was, of course, freed, and a few weeks later the matter was fully investigated.

In the course of the trial Nwa Udaw Uko stated on oath:

"About three years ago Etesin sold my brother-in-law, Umana Isong, to a man whose name I do not know. Many years ago he had already sold him to someone in the Opobo District. Umana ran back to our town, and three years ago accused sold him again. We do not know where he is now. The reason accused gave for selling him the second time was that Umana had committed adultery with Etesin's brother's wife. A long time ago accused also sold my first husband. I do not know where the latter was sent. He has never been seen again."

Akpan Nkana (witness for prosecutor), sworn, stated:

"About three years ago accused sold Umana Isong to some place. Since that time Umana has never returned to his town. He was a relative of accused's. A long while before he had been sold, it was said by his own father, but escaped and came back to Iton, his native place. During the time of the war at Ikot Ebokk accused sold Nwa Udaw Uko's husband, Eduok Adiaha

Ekkpo by name. He has never returned. I am a relative of the woman."

Etesin stated:

"Once, a long time ago, I went to another country to get Idiong. On my return I heard that Umana Isong's father had sold him. I said nothing, but went to my house. Umana escaped and came back. The people who had bought him came and caught him again. This was a long time ago. I cannot mention the number of years. It was at the time that his sister, Adiaha Isong, whom I am calling as a witness, was in the Fatting-house. She has now borne five children. I never sold Eduok Adiaha Ekkpo."

Question by Nwa Udaw Uko: "Who sold my husband?"

Answer: "Essien did."

Adiaha Isong (called as witness for accused) stated on oath:

"It is three years ago since accused sold my brother Umana Isong. About a year before that accused had also sold my elder brother Eduok Adiaha Ekkpo."

Question by accused: "Who sold Umana Isong first of all?"

Answer by Adiaha: "My father did."

Udaw Eka Etuk Ikpa (called as witness for accused), sworn, stated:

"It is three years ago since Etesin sold Umana Isong. He also sold Eduok Adiaha Ekkpo several years ago. I am a relative of Umana Isong's. Nearly everyone in our family was sold as a slave."

Question by accused: "Did not Isong Akpabio sell your half-brother Akpan Isong?"

Answer: "No. You sold him also."

Not a single witness could be brought forward to testify in favour of the accused, and, as a result of trying to extort Nwa Udaw Uko's latest piccan from her, and inducing the clerk to imprison her until she consented to give it up, he himself was awarded two years' hard labour.

After Court, according to my husband's usual practice, all prisoners were called before him to ask if they had any complaint to make. Besides the one whose case is given above, there were five women prisoners, and of these all but one were found to have been sentenced without due cause.

The case of the second on the list, Ekkpo Udia of Ekott Ibokk, was perhaps the most characteristic. She had been convicted before the Native Court by a council of chiefs and sentenced to two months' imprisonment with hard labour for the terrible crime of having put her daughter into the Fatting-house without first obtaining her husband's permission, and for not taking her out again immediately on learning his opinion that she should wait for some months before starting the course of feeding up, for which, by the way, the mother provided nearly all the necessary food.

MARRIAGE PROBLEMS

FROM a case brought before the Ikotobo Native Court it would appear that among the Ubium Ibibios the death penalty was inflicted upon a woman who married a man from another town. In the course of his evidence the defendant, Okonnor Asom, head chief of Ikotobo, stated on oath:

"Three years ago Etuk Udaw Nwa Mbiam came and told me that the plaintiff, Obot Udo, refused to remain as a wife with her former husband Akpan Idui, and had said to the latter, 'If you can find a new husband for me to marry, I will wed him instead of you; for I would rather be a sort of sister to you than remain as a wife.'

"On learning this I said to Etuk Udaw, 'If you think that plaintiff would like to marry me, please bring her to my house so that I can see her.' After four days, he brought the woman to Ubium market, and called me to come and look at her. I did so, and she told Etuk Udaw, 'I should like you to take me to defendant's house.' Three days later, therefore, he brought her with her sister Ema and, Udaw Etuk Ukpon. When they came I gave them palm wine. They drank, and plaintiff said, 'I am willing to marry you.' I answered, 'Very well. I will come to your town, Ndukpo-Isi, and see your former husband and your mother. If they agree, I will refund the dowry.'

"I went according to promise. Akpan Idui said, 'If the plaintiff agrees to marry you, you can repay the dowry to me, and after that she will be to me as a stepdaughter.'

"On the same day I went to the mother and spoke of marriage, but she answered, 'The townspeople of Ndukpo-Isi have a law that should a girl from their town marry a stranger she must die.'

"Next morning the mother came to my house and said: 'Akpan Idui has quarrelled with me, asking, "Why have you prevented the girl from marrying a new husband, so that the dowry might be repaid to us?"'

"Five days later a messenger came from Akpan to call me to Ndukpo-Isi. On my arrival he said, 'Plaintiff's mother has now agreed for you to refund the dowry.'

"I therefore took manillas to the value of thirteen goats, and on that same day gave one fathom of cloth and one gown to the girl's mother, saying, 'Take and give these to your daughter as a sign that she is my wife.'

"After two weeks plaintiff and Ekkpo Manga came to my house. The woman slept there for two nights, after which she went back to her mother. Two weeks later Udaw Etuk Udaw came to me and said, 'Have you heard what has happened to your wife? 'I answered, 'No.' He said, 'Udaw Afaha Ama told her that if she continued married to you she would not be allowed to five.'"

From this case, and the still more horrible penalty exacted, even to the present day, among the Okkobbor people as related in another place, [24] it would appear that the regulation as to endogamy was enforced against women marrying out of their own town or clan; but no trace of any custom restricting men in like manner has come to our notice.

Many indications seem to point to the probability that among the tribes of this district communal marriage was practised at no very distant date.

Once when we were about to leave Okon Ekkpo (Jamestown) a deputation of chiefs under the leadership of Efa Abassi of Ibaka came up to say that they wished to go back to the old custom by which not the husband alone, but his "age class" or "company" might claim damages from the co-respondent in case of unfaithfulness on the part of the wife of a member.

This custom of claiming common damages for infidelity would seem to indicate a former state of affairs in which wives of members were regarded as the common property of the whole "society." In such a case the idea which prevails, not in this district only, but also among the Ekoi and many other tribes, that a wife's unfaithfulness entails misfortune, sickness and even death upon her husband, may in earlier days have extended until it was supposed to affect the "age class" as a whole.

Should a husband fall ill, his first idea is to suspect his wife as the probable cause. The case of Nka Anang, heard in Awa Court, on August Ist, 1913, is typical of many. In this the complainant stated that he had fallen sick, and, thinking that the illness must have been sent as a consequence of his wife's unfaithfulness, taxed her with this: on which the woman confessed to having three lovers.

As will be found related under "Burial Customs" (p. 206), the oracle was usually consulted after the death of a chief in order to discover whether this had been brought about through infidelity on the part of one of his wives. When the answer was in the affirmative, the unfortunate woman charged with the crime was either entombed alive or impaled above the grave of her dead lord. [25]

*   *   *   *   *

Two things arouse the hatred of Ibibio women beyond all else, namely when one steals from another the love of a husband, or when one wife is fruitful and another barren. In such a case the favoured woman is always in grave danger; for her childless rival will usually go to any lengths in order to destroy her. Many such seek out a juju man or famous witch-wife, and at the price of all their possessions buy themselves into some terrible "affinity," such as crocodile or water snake. Once capable of assuming this were-form, the jealous woman is supposed to build herself a house beneath the river, and when all is ready, lure her rival to the spot on some pretext or other, and there drown her.

A case showing the savage jealousy of a childless wife to one more favoured was reported by an Efik woman informant. Owing to our sudden removal from the district the facts are unconfirmed, but even so they are so typical of the state of feeling among childless women that it seems worth while to give them.

A man had two wives, the last married of whom showed signs that a babe was about to be born to her, before hope of such a thing was vouchsafed to the elder wife. One night, therefore, the latter took a small penknife, like the cruel mother in the old northern ballad, [26] and crept into the room where her happy rival lay sleeping. So savagely did she slash at the victim of her spite that the unborn child was killed and the prospective mother died not long after. The murderess is reported to be still undergoing punishment.

So rooted is this hatred on the part of barren women that they are said to wreak it even upon the children of dead rivals. Such a story was told by a very old Ibibio woman:

"Once a man had two wives, one of whom bore him a fine piccan, while the other was barren. After a few years the fruitful woman died, leaving her son to the care of her fellow wife. Now it chanced that the latter, whose name was Afia, went out to her farm to gather the ripening corn, but lo! birds were eating it. So she hired someone to make snares for her and set them in the farm for the protection of the crops.

"Next day she went to visit these and found a bird caught in one of them. Its plumage was very gay and fine, so she determined not to kill it, but made a cage of split palm stem, and therein bore it home.

"When market-day came round, before setting out she called to the small boy, her stepson, and said, 'Look after the bird while I am gone.' No sooner had she left the house, however, than the child set the cage upon the grass, and took the bird in his hand, whispering to himself, 'I wonder if such a small bird is old enough to fly away.' So saying he unclosed his hand a little, on which the bird flew up and settled upon a plantain leaf outside. At first the boy was frightened, but comforted himself saying, 'I do not think it can fly far. It is so small. Surely I shall soon be able to catch it again." Then he ran out and tried his best to do so, but the bird spread its wings and flew away into the bush, where it was hidden amid the dark trees so that the boy could not follow.

"When the stepmother came back, she went straight up to the cage and looked at it, but saw no bird. So she asked, 'Where is the bird which I told you to guard during my absence?'

"Tremblingly the small child answered, 'I did not think that he could fly away, so I took him out to see if he had yet learnt to move his wings!' To this the cruel stepmother replied angrily, 'Go out and recapture my bird. Without him do not dare to come back to the house.' Shaking with fear the little one answered, 'The bird has gone so far! I cannot catch it any more.'

"On this the stepmother seized him and beat him very cruelly, hitting him on the side so that he died. She did not want her husband to know that she had killed his son, and therefore took the little body and hid it under the bed. Then she began to cook 'chop,' not knowing that a neighbour had witnessed what she had done.

"When the husband came back from mimbo-cutting he said: 'Bring "chop"': on which the woman brought what she had prepared and placed it before him. Then he said, 'Call my son to come and eat with me.' She answered, 'The boy has already eaten.' On this the man fell to. After his hunger was a little satisfied he said, 'My son always "chops" with me. Call the boy. I will not finish without him': to which she replied, 'He has gone out to play.' So the husband said, 'Very well, I will keep some of the food until he returns.'

"A long time passed and yet the boy did not come, so the man asked further: 'Where is it that my son has gone to play?' To this the wife answered, 'I do not know.' After waiting yet some time the man said, 'I must go myself to seek him.' So he set out and searched all around, but could not find the child. On his way back he saw the old neighbour sitting by her door, and asked her, 'Have you seen my son?' She answered, 'Have you asked your wife?' To which he replied, 'Yes, and she told me that he had gone out to play.'

"The old woman said, 'I heard what she said to the boy about the bird which he let fly. Also I watched her kill him and hide him under the bed. Go, therefore, and look at the bottom of your wife's bed and see what you find there.'

"In silence the man did as she bade, and there found the little dead form. Gently he carried it out to his own room, then called to his wife and asked, 'Who did this thing? Whoever has done it must wake up my son again for me.' The woman replied, 'If you want to have the boy again, give back my bird which he let fly.'

"On this the man sent to fetch his wife's father and mother, that they might see what their daughter had done to the dead woman's child. On their coming they said, 'Never have we known such a thing as this. Do, therefore, what you choose with the woman.'

"On that the husband turned to his wife and asked, 'Can you give me back my son?' To this she replied, 'Get back my bird, and perhaps I may think of bringing back the child of the woman whom I hated.' This so angered the husband that he slew her. After which he went out to the bush and hanged himself: for he did not care to live now that his only child was dead, since there was none to bury him or pour out the ghost offerings over his grave."

A terrible revenge sometimes taken by discarded wives upon husbands who have rejected them was confided to me by an Efik woman.

"When a man took a dislike to his wife without cause," she said, "he used to drive her forth from his house, giving merely, as sufficient reason, that he did not want her any more. Often the woman would cling to him, praying that he would relent and not send her away. Sometimes the neighbours, knowing her to be innocent of any fault, would come and beg him to take her back. Should entreaties still prove vain, in the olden days, unless she cared to seek another husband, she had no course but to go sadly away, alone and outcast; since by marriage she had lost all part or lot in her father's property, and was no longer considered of her former family, but as belonging only to that of her husband. Driven thence, therefore, she was without refuge, alone and empty of heart, for the husband kept all children whom she had borne him."

In such a case the only way "to bring repentance to her lover, and wring his bosom" was "to die"--not alone, since that would have been but a matter of indifference to her callous lord, but in such a way as might indeed "wring his bosom." Evening after evening, therefore, the outcast wife. would creep round the compound whence she had been thrust, waiting until chance came to inveigle one of her own piccans out from its sleeping-place. When she had succeeded in this, she bore the little one down to the river, and, standing on the brink, gazed out over the swift-flowing water. Cold, deep and black, it swept by, tenanted by crocodiles, water snakes and a hundred unknown terrors; yet to the outcast less terrible than the life which would henceforth be hers. So with a bitter cry she fell forward, as a log falls, the babe tight clasped to her breast, and the cruel current sucked them under, to be washed up, perchance, on some far-off beach, or seen no more of men.

Next morning when the husband woke and found his piccan gone he mourned for its loss, and, perhaps, for its sake, cast a thought of regret to the woman whom he had driven away, wishing that he had been less harsh, so that their child might still have played in the sunshine. Then, when his turn came to cross that other river, and wife and babe were found awaiting him upon its farther shore, he might, it is thought, be moved to kindliness and take her once more for his own, so that she need no longer dwell husbandless and deserted in the world of shadows.

Not long ago a case occurred in which a man, grown weary of his wife, decided to put her away. The woman could not bear to leave him, and as she was young and pretty the pitying neighbours advised her to dance once more before her husband. She did so, and when the dance was ended and he still stood unrelenting, ran and threw her arms about him, crying: "I will not let you go! I will not let you go!" Alas! Her frail arms had no power to restrain the errant fancy or bring back to her the lost affection of her fickle lord.

LOVE PHILTRES AND MAGIC

ONE morning, just as we were leaving Okon Ekkpo (Jamestown), a deputation of chiefs came to lay a case of some interest before my husband. The head wife of one of them had accused a fellow wife of attempting to administer a "love potion" to their common lord, the effect of which would be to draw his affection from all others to the giver alone. The potion had been bought from a noted witch-doctor of the neighbourhood. In this case the magician in question was a woman, young and singularly attractive in appearance.

At first sight the crime did not seem very heinous, but it transpired that love potions are by no means harmless, since they contain small portions of a powerful poison, repeated doses of which are said not only to affect the brain and render the recipient incapable of normal judgment, but even to bring death in the end. The principal ingredients in these philtres are the hearts of chickens pounded up to a smooth paste, together with leaves thought to contain magical qualities. It is not without significance that among the Ibibios, save when administered in "medicine" intended to weaken the will or destroy the courage of the recipient, the hearts and livers of chickens are carefully avoided as food, since it is thought that those who partake will become "chicken-hearted" in consequence.

In order to render the charm efficacious it is necessary to draw forth the soul of some person and imprison it amid fresh-plucked herbs in an earthen pot never before used. The vessel is then hung above a slow fire, and, as the leaves dry up, the body of the man or woman chosen for the purpose is said to wither away.

In the present case, a fellow wife, Antikka by name, was the victim chosen, and when my husband asked whether any evil consequences had been thought to result, the complainant drew forth the woman, remarking:

"Our District Commissioner can see for himself. Formerly Antikka was a very fresh woman, plump and beautiful. Now that her soul has been drawn into the pot and withered by slow fire it is plain to see that she has become dry and sapless."

The woman was very pale, of mixed blood, and it was easy to see from her drawn face and terror-stricken air that, however foolish such a story sounds to twentieth-century ears, it was no idle tale to her.

In view of the importance attached to such cases by no less an authority than Dr. Wallis Budge, of the British Museum, it may be well to give the proceedings in full.

During the course of the trial a fellow wife named Ikwaw Eyo stated on oath:

"I was in my house when Ikwaw came and said,

We are all three the wives of one husband. Let us make medicine that our husband may not love his other wife, Antikka.' Afterwards I went to him and reported: 'Ikwaw has asked me to join her in preparing a love philtre so that you will not be able to care for any other wives.'

"Another time the same woman came to me and said, 'Aret knows all about magic leaves.' After this she asked me to come into the house where the magician was, but when the latter saw me she said, 'It is not a good thing to have called Ikwaw Eyo into the presence of the medicine. She may tell her husband about it.'

"All this also I reported, and told, too, that Aret had bidden Ikwaw buy a little clay bowl in the marketplace of the value of four wires. This she did, and later, when all was prepared, they asked me, 'Whose soul do you think we should call into the pot?' I answered, 'I do not know.' On this Aret said, 'Let her alone. To-day we will grind the medicine and afterwards we can settle whose soul it will be best to call.'

"Next Ikwaw was sent out to get an egg. She begged me to bring one also, and I went to Antikka and asked her for one, which she gave, and I in turn handed it to Ikwaw. Then Aret and she made the medicine, and called Antikka's soul. Long they called, very softly, and in words which I could not understand. After a while they sent me out, bidding me fetch some yellow ogokk powder, and on my return Aret said, 'We have already called Antikka's soul into the pot.' Ikwaw then begged Aret to call our husband's soul also before the juju, but the medicine woman said, 'If I should do this the soul of your husband would go wandering, and he himself would fall sick of his body.'

"Ikwaw told me that Aret had also stated, 'We may not beat this medicine in one of the fu-fu mortars. Should we do this the vessel could not be used again.' Ikwaw then sent me to bring one of the old mats from before Antikka's house. I refused, but afterwards fetched one in secret from her own house instead of that of Antikka. Aret gave me a piece of root to hang up over my hearth, but Ikwaw advised her not to let me have it, as should our husband come to my house and see it hanging in the fireplace, he would be sure to ask about it, and I should then very likely tell him of the secret thing they had done. In my presence Aret also said to Ikwaw:

"'When you bring your husband water in which to wash in the morning take a little of the liquid from out the pot of medicine, and mix with the fresh water. Also spread some upon the side of the bowl, and at night before you go to lie in his bed, rub some of this juju over your own arms, feet and neck.'

"Later Ikwaw bore the pot of medicine into her bedroom and I went away, but that same day our husband went to visit her. He saw the medicine and carried it off to his house. Next day he called a meeting of the chiefs, then summoned Aret and Ikwaw before them and asked, 'What sort of medicine is this which you have been making?' They answered, 'It is a love philtre.' So the chiefs said that the case must be brought to Court."

Ikwaw stated on oath:

"One day I asked Aret to come and give medicine to my little daughter who was sick. About this time Eyo said to me, 'Akon Abassi, our fellow wife, is making love philtres for our husband. That is why he loves her more than us. Let us therefore find someone who can make such medicine for us also.'

"I answered, 'I have no money'; but she said, 'I will bring some.' Later she brought five shillings, which she asked me to give to Aret. I showed the money to the latter, who said, 'I cannot accept it, as I do not know why it is given.' Afterwards Eyo, came secretly to the back of my house and said, 'Arrange with Aret about the love philtre.' Later I asked Aret to come and see me again. We met Eyo outside the door of my house. She asked Aret, 'Have you brought the medicine?' Aret answered 'Yes.' Eyo questioned further, 'What must one do with it?' Aret replied, 'Bring a fu-fu mortar.' This Eyo did. The magic bark was laid in it, and at her request I beat this to powder. When all was prepared I asked Eyo to take the medicine to her house. She said, 'I cannot, because no one is sick there, and should our husband see it and ask the reason for my having it I should have nothing to say in excuse.'"

Only a short time ago an epidemic of such "love poisoning" was said to have broken out in Calabar, and to have caused the death of many chiefs.

The following case in which a love philtre also figures came before the Native Court at Awa on April 25th, 1913. In this the prosecutor, Ayana Etuk Udaw, sworn, stated:

"About a year ago I went to Ikot Etobo where one Udofia Nwa by name told me that Akpan Nka had asked him to make a medicine to give to my wife Owo, so that she might leave me and go to him. Udofia also said that he had given the medicine to Akpan Nka."

Udofia Nwa stated on oath:

"About a year ago the accused asked me to make medicine for him. I inquired to whom he was going to give it, and he said it was for the prosecutor's wife Owo, to cause her to leave her present husband and come to him. I made the medicine. Afterwards prosecutor came to my country and I asked him if his wife was still with him. He said, 'No, she has gone away.' On hearing this I reported that the accused had bought medicine from me with the intention of taking the woman from him by this means. First the accused had said that he wanted it for his sister, and afterwards that it was for prosecutor's wife."

The accused stated

"About a year ago I asked the witness Udofia Nwa to make a medicine for me. He asked to whom I was going to give it, and I mentioned my sister, who is living at Afia Nsitt. I wanted her to take the medicine so that she should return to me and I should then be able to give her in marriage to anyone whom I chose. I did not mention the name of prosecutor's wife, nor have I given medicine to the woman."

A third case in which a love philtre played a part, came before the Court at Idua Oron. This time it was a jealous mistress who sought to administer the potion. The account is given by a woman well known to all those concerned.

George Offong, a former Native Court clerk, had married two wives at his own town, Okatt. When he was transferred to Idua as clerk of court, he met an Oron woman named Emiene whom he induced to come to his house. After a short time he sent to fetch his two wives, and one came while the other remained behind. Now the one who answered his call was his best-loved wife, Etuk Udaw by name, and before long it was clear to the Oron woman that Offong cared far more for the new-comer than for herself. This angered her, and she determined to steal away his affection so that he might be led to divorce his wife.

With this end in view she got together her most valued possessions, and went to a famous witch-doctor to purchase a love philtre. The necessary potion was given, and she was instructed as to the rites to be carried out in order to ensure its efficacy. For this she had to go alone to a waste place, and there, hidden from all eyes, carry out the prescribed ritual. While thus engaged a friend of her lover chanced to pass through the bush, near the spot which she had chosen.

Attracted by light and sound in so lonely a place the man crept near and hid behind some trees, where unseen and unsuspected, he could witness everything. Only when the last rite was finished and the woman, exhausted by the frenzy of her petition, lay prone upon the ground did he steal away to tell Offong what he had seen. In consequence both men made investigations and succeeded in learning all that was to be known.

Not till long after dark had fallen did Emiene creep back to her lover's house. When she appeared before him he charged her with the carrying out of evil rites in order to turn his love away from Etuk Udaw and transfer it to herself. She denied all knowledge of this, saying, "I never did any such thing." To this Offong replied, "There is a man who witnessed all that you have done. Also we know from whom you bought the medicine, and the price which you paid."

On hearing this Emiene said, "Send for this man that I may know who accuses me."

When the witness came forward and told of the very place where she had practised the charm, and of all she had said and done there, as also the name of the witch-doctor from whom the love philtre had been bought, she realised that further denial was useless; so hung her head and said never a word. After the accuser had gone the poor woman held out her arms toward Offong and pleaded that what she had done was but because it was hard to live in his house day by day and see another woman preferred before herself. She entreated, therefore, that he would forgive her and let her stay on as before, but he answered, "That cannot be. I must bring the matter before court."

So this was done, with the result that the members pronounced her guilty and sentenced her to three months' imprisonment.

Afterwards Offong would never see her again.

Other magic rites in frequent use are practised by jealous men or women to wither up the vital powers of those who have fallen under their displeasure and prevent such from the procreation of offspring. Such a case happened not long ago and is thus related by Udaw of Ikot Atako.

"A woman of Ikot Akpan Udaw, by name Adiaha Ntokk, was given by her parents in marriage to a fellow townsman named Udaw Nka Nta. For some years she lived quietly in her hus-band's house and bore him two babes. Afterwards she grew weary of him, and seeing another man who pleased her better, said to Nka Nta:

"'I am tired of you, and have seen a man whom I like better. He is willing to repay the dowry which you gave to my parents, so I shall leave you and go to him.'

"Now Nka Nta loved this woman with so strong a passion that, because of it, he cared for no other wife; so he begged her not to leave him. She, however, only laughed at his entreaties, gathered together her possessions, and prepared to go to the house of her new lover.

"When Udaw Nka Nta saw that she had determined to leave him he went before the juju and made sacrifice, calling upon the spirit to hear his prayer. Then he came back and stood before the woman and said:

"'Since you will no longer be my wife you shall henceforth be barren. Never shall you bear a babe to another man.'

"For the moment Adiaha Ntokk was startled, but she soon rallied and answered with a laugh and a toss of the head, 'You are not Abassi to give or withhold children.'

"To this the man replied, 'I know very well that of myself I have no power, but the spell I have wrought is a very strong one, and in time you will see whether or no my words are vain. Once again I tell you, if you leave my house for that of another you will never bear piccan more.'

"In spite of this Adiaha persisted, and went to her new lover. Yet the curse held, and though she lived with him for several years, Eka Abassi sent no babe to their hearth.

"After a time the faithless wife again grew weary and thought: 'I will seek out a new husband by whom I may bear a child, since this one is of no use to me.' So she married a third man, named Anam Okut, and still lives at Afa Eket; but the juju which her first husband put upon her yet holds. Never a babe has been born to her, and no new husband will take to his house a wife so accursed."

Another method of bringing barrenness upon those against whom a grudge is harboured came out in a case heard at Idua Oron on July 14th, 1913. In this a man, Ekpenyon by name, accused his wife Isong Edigi Owo of invoking the great Mbiam juju, Ita Brinyan, or as it is sometimes called Atabli Inyan, against him.

The plaintiff stated on oath:

"Three weeks ago I gave my wife thirty wires and asked her to go and buy fish and palm oil for me. She took the wires, but when later I sent to ask for what she had bought she answered that she had nothing. I therefore went to her house and inquired why she had not purchased the fish. First she would not speak, then answered that she had only bought oil. I caught hold of her and drew her out of the house, telling her to go and buy the fish. She refused, whereupon I pushed her and she prepared to fight me. I struck her and she caught hold of me . . . so I threw her down, and my other wife ran out to part us. Afterwards Isong Edigi went out and cut leaves, praying that no other child might be born from me, and that Ita Brinyan might kill me. To make the curse more sure she washed a certain part of her body, then threw the water before my door, crying out that I must never more become the father of a babe. She asserted that while we were fighting I had wounded that part of her, and that this was why she called upon the juju against me."

Thereupon the Court asked accused: "Did you hold the leaves in your two hands?"

Answer: "Yes."

Question: "When a person holds leaves in both hands and calls upon the name of Atabli Inyan, what is meant?"

To this the accused refused to reply, whereon one of the Court Members, deputed to speak for the others, rose and said:

"Atabli Inyan is the strongest of all Mbiams. He dwells by the waterside and beneath the water. Had the woman not meant to invoke this juju against her husband she would not thus have held the leaves in her two hands while calling upon his name."

Another case in which a magic potion figures came up before the same Native Court on July 15th, 1913. In this the plaintiff, Anwa Ese, stated:

"Defendant went to a medicine man named Umo Ekkpe, and asked for a juju which would kill me or destroy my reason, so that he might be able to marry my wife. The chiefs of our town questioned him about the matter in the presence of several people and he never denied it."

Abassi Anse, brother of plaintiff, sworn, stated

"The accused went to Umo Ekkpe, to get a medicine with which to kill my brother or make him mad, so that the latter's wife should become his own."

Ekpenyong Ata stated on oath:

"I heard that accused went to buy a love medicine to give to complainant's wife in order that the woman might love him."

Okon Udaw stated:

"I admit that I went to buy a medicine from Umo Ekkpe, but it is only a love potion. It cannot kill anyone. I wished to give the medicine to complainant's wife, because I love her and do not know whether she loves me or not."

Some Ibibio women know the secret of a "magic" which will attract a husband's love to them alone, and guard the thoughts of their lords from straying to rivals. The following information was gleaned from women informants, one of whom stated:

"A very famous medicine is one that is only known to witches, and must be purchased at a great price from a witch-doctor.

This is never used save when a woman has grown tired of her husband and wishes to rid herself of him in order to marry another man. It is a terrible potion which, once administered, goes straight to the head and destroys all will-power, placing the victim under the control of her who has administered it. So soon as a man has eaten or drunk of the fatal mixture the faithless wife has but to say 'Now go,' and, no matter how strong, young or wealthy he may be the husband must rise at once, and, abandoning all his possessions and everything that life holds dear, go straight down to the river, there to drown himself--leaving his cruel witch-wife free to marry another man.

"Some men know how to make a medicine which will turn to them the heart of any woman whom they may desire, and also kill her former husband, should she be married. Some possess the juju Ibokk Ima, which they place in a little niche in the mud wall above the lintel. To this object, which is usually in the form of a ball made of twisted tie-tie, a cord is fastened, and at night-time the man goes and pulls it gently seven times, calling upon the name of the woman and crying, 'Come! I want you! Come! I want you!' until she rises in sleep, even from her husband's side, and is forced to go to the house of the one who thus summons her. Arrived at the door, still in her sleep, she knocks softly, and her lover opens and leads her within. . . . When she goes back to her husband next morning perhaps he will ask her, 'Where have you been?' She is quite dazed and knows not what to say, so to avert suspicion, usually answers, 'I come from my mother's place.'"

A very old woman, strongly suspected of possessing uncanny powers, said one day:

"The juju Ikoruben can make doors fly open before a man at night-time so that such a one can enter unseen and unheard, and bear off any sleeping woman in his arms. Afterwards he can carry her back in the same way, and the woman never know what has been done to her. Should she chance to wake and find herself in a strange room she will cry, 'Where am I; afar from my house, in that of a stranger?' Usually, however, she falls asleep once more and does not wake up again until she finds herself back in her own home. Then, if she tells anyone of the strange dream which she had in the night, the friend in whom she confides raises a warning finger and says, 'Hush! Tell no one! It is the juju Ikoruben or Ibokk Ima that has taken you, and it is not good for your husband to know of the matter.'

The juju Etuk Nwan is also said to confer the power of passing invisibly through locked doors and thus entering houses at midnight. By its help men are said to obtain the favours of women who had scorned them by daylight, and also to steal whatever goods they may happen to covet. Such a case was brought before my husband in the Native Court at Oron, where an Akaiya man was accused of having practised the juju to the great loss of all his townsfolk.

In order to ensure efficacy for this particular "magic" the presence of a confederate is needed. The latter must stand outside the house which is about to be burgled, holding in his hands the skull of a sheep or of an "Ebett," sometimes called the "sleeping antelope." Should the attention of the watcher be distracted, or should he lay down the skull even for a moment, the spell would be broken, and the thief, no longer invisible, is liable to be seized. Strange as such a belief may seem, it is no more remarkable than that which survived until lately in our own land, namely, that a candle fastened into a hand cut from the body of a murderer as it swung from the gallows-tree would confer the same immunity upon burglars. It is somewhat singular that a belief similar to that of the Ibibios obtains among

Zulus, only with these latter the skull of another species of antelope is used.

The secrets of all "invisible jujus" were thought to have been confided to mortals by evil spirits, whose underground dwellings, according to local belief, are entered through the curiously shaped ant-hills which abound in this part of the world, and before which small sacrificial bowls and other offerings may usually be seen.

The origin of the "invisible juju" is given in the following legend which, in a slightly different form. was also found among the Ekoi.

"Once, long ago, a hunter went out into the bush to snare animals. He set his traps, and then climbed up into a tree to watch for prey. Near the place was an ant-hill, which in this part of the country is supposed to be the home of evil spirits.

"While the hunter sat watching, safely screened from view amid the branches, he saw seven such spirits come out. They all wore human form, and one of them bore a vessel full of juju. This he sprinkled over himself and his six companions, rubbing it well over all their bodies, until one by one they became invisible; but before quite fading away, the last of them hid the bowl of medicine in a secret place.

"After a while the hunter climbed down, took out the basin, rubbed its contents over himself, and then, assured of invisibility, followed the spirits.

The way led to the market-place, and arrived there he saw the seven genii and they saw him. They wondered greatly how this 'earth child' had become possessed of the invisible juju, so they said to one another, 'Let us go back and see whether our medicine is safe.'

"When these evil beings reached their home once more they searched for the bowl of juju, but could not find it. On this they grew very angry and threatened to kill the hunter, who by now had hastened back to his hiding-place in the tree. After searching a long time the spirits looked up and saw him there. Then they called out:

'Is it you who have stolen our medicine?'

The hunter owned to having found the bowl, whereon the evil beings said:

"'If you will come down and give it back to us we swear to give you a portion for yourself.'

"On this the man climbed down, took the vessel from the place where he had hidden it, and gave it back to its owners. The latter put a part aside for him saying:

"'This will confer great power upon you, for by its use you may become rich. Only take care not to use it too often, lest you should get into trouble.'

"Before re-entering the ant-hill one of the genii turned toward the hunter and added:

"'Should you tell anyone the secret of the medicine or of its use we shall come for you and kill you.'

"The man promised to keep the secret, and went home well pleased. After awhile he began to grow rich, for by means of the invisible juju he could enter into any house and steal whatsoever he chose.

"At last the townsfolk rose up, called a meeting of chiefs, and asked:

"'Whence does this man get all his cows, goats and sheep, with money and many rich things, while we grow poor through continual thefts?'

"The chiefs called the hunter before them and asked him to give the reason for his changed circumstances. At first he refused to reply, but they said:

"'If you do not answer we will put you to death.'

On this the man feared greatly, and at length confessed how he had become possessed of the power. Hardly had he finished than he fell down dead."

There is a very efficacious way by which a woman may enlist the help of the evil spirits who dwell within ant-hills. This also is one of the woman's mysteries, which must be carefully guarded from the knowledge of man. In order to carry out the rites a woman should go herself, or send a magician of her own sex, hired for the purpose, at about the time of the full moon. Then, standing so that her shadow falls upon the mound, she must recite certain incantations proper to the occasion. After awhile some small creature will be seen to creep out near the base of the hill. This must be caught and enclosed in a little receptacle prepared in readiness. After binding it round with strips of cloth, preferably white, it should be worn beneath the garments, and will confer magical powers upon its owner, both for good and ill.

Though far less elaborate, this rite is in some ways like that by which Kedah ladies seek to obtain possession of that strange little familiar the "pelsit," so inimitably described in the fascinating pages of "In Court and Kampong." [27]

"Polong and pelsit are but other names for bajang, the latter is chiefly used in the State of Kedah, where it is considered rather chic to have a pelsit. A Kedah lady on one occasion, eulogising the advantage of possessing a familiar spirit (she said that amongst other things it gave her absolute control over her husband and the power of annoying people who offended her), thus described the method of securing this useful ally:

"'You go out,' she said, 'on the night before the full moon and stand with your back to the moon and your face to an ant-hill, so that your shadow falls on the ant-hill. Then you recite certain jampi (incantations), and bending forward try to embrace your shadow. If you fail try again seven times, repeating more incantations. If not successful go the next night and make a further effort, and the night after if necessary--three nights in all. If you cannot then catch your shadow wait till the same day on the following month and renew the attempt. Sooner or later you will succeed, and as you stand there in the brilliance of the moonlight, you will see that you have drawn your shadow into yourself, and your body will never again cast a shade. Go home, and in the night, whether sleeping or waking, the form of a child will appear before you and put out its tongue; that seize, and it will remain while the rest of the child disappears. In a little while the tongue will turn into something that breathes, a small animal, reptile or insect, and when you see the creature has life put it in a bottle and the pelsit is yours.'"

A still more gruesome recipe for securing this familiar is to "go to the graveyard at night and dig up the body of a first-born child whose mother was also first-born . . . carry it to an ant-hill in the open ground and there dandle it (di-timang). After a little while, when the child shrieks and lolls its tongue out (terjerlir lidah-nya) bite off its tongue and carry it home. Then obtain a coco-nut shell . . . carry it to a place where three roads meet, light a fire and heat the shell till oil exudes, dip the child's tongue in the oil and bury it in the heart of the three cross roads (hati sempang tiga). Leave it untouched for three nights, then dig it up and you will find that it has turned into a pelsit." [28]

It is to propitiate the evil spirits which dwell beneath ant-hills that little huts are so often built above them, usually hung round with pieces of white cloth or other votive offerings.

As in so many stories of white magic among the ancients whether carried out with the object of acquiring wealth, regaining health, or inducing victory to crown a warrior's arms, the aid of a faithful wife is necessary for the success of most charms.

One of the most fantastic of jujus is called "Kukubarakpa." There are many magic rites for the obtaining of riches, but that of the python (asaba) is more powerful than all.

These magic creatures live in creeks or rivers, and are credited, according to popular belief, with bearing a great shining stone in the head, much as was "the toad ugly and venomous" among ourselves not very long ago. Many legends exist as to the power of this gem, by virtue of which riches beyond the dreams of avarice may be conferred upon those who enter the "python affinity," or purchase a share in its magic. People who long for wealth go to a juju man known to possess familiars such as these, and bargain with him for the sale of one.

The first step is to swallow a thread seven fathoms long "as a sign of the animal." Later, a tiny pad, in all save size like those which carriers wear upon the head beneath their loads, must also be gulped down. It is upon this little cushion that, when the rites are over and the thread has become metamorphosed into a snake, the reptile rests, "so as not to injure the body of its owner by pressing directly upon it."

One rule must be strictly observed. The first money gained "by the power of the snake" may not be used directly for the enjoyment of its possessors, but must be brought before the priest. Should this rule be forgotten, the man who thus made too great haste to be rich would die at once. Nothing could save him.

It was confided to us that the full law of the juju is as follows: The man who bears the snake within him goes home and tells the matter to that one of his wives whom he can trust above all others. Then together they build a small "secret court" within their compound entered by two doors, one of which opens into the room set aside for the private use of the husband. and the other into that of the trusted wife.

In the midst of the hidden court a great earthen pot or bowl must be set filled with fresh spring water. Into this the couple throw leaves, together with roots and bark of magic potency, provided by the juju man for the purpose. Afterwards, with the point of a spear, a hole is driven through the bottom of the pot by which the water that is within might sink into the breast of Isong, our mother. Down and down it sinks, making by magic a channel right through to the riverside.

It is fatal to attempt to carry out this juju during the time of storms; for thunder and lightning would render it of no avail. December, January and February are the best months for carrying out the rites, since that is the season of Isu Akariku, i.e. the Face of the Fog. Beware of lightning, for Obumo is much to be feared in matters of magic; since he is a god very jealous of all powers which seem as if seeking to rival him in might.

When the pot has been placed in position during calm weather in the midst of the hidden court, after a hole has been driven through the bottom, the husband must wait patiently until the hour of low tide. So soon as this is reached he goes to his room, locks the door by which it communicates with the secret place, and sends all his "boys" away, saying, "Should anyone ask for me tell them I am away from home." Then he lays himself down upon his bed and falls into a deep sleep, while his trusted wife stays on guard by the magic pot, a fresh egg poised in her hand.

The woman may not lift her eyes from the bowl even for a second. So soon as the tide turns water begins to flow up and swirl round at the bottom. This is, however, not yet the time for the magic to work. At the exact moment of high tide, as the water rushes through, for one instant the head of a python is seen within the pot. At once she must fling the egg so that it strikes the reptile. Then the water rises and rises till it pours over the earthen rim and overflows the whole yard. When the woman sees this, she knows that her part is done for the time; so slips softly away into her room, where she locks the door and lies down to sleep.

This juju can only be carried out by a loving and faithful wife, for should the watcher at any time have had another lover her thoughts would certainly turn to him and she would miss the moment for throwing in the egg; in which case the husband would never more wake from his sleep. Not till next morning may the door of the secret court be opened. When this is done it will be found full of thousands of wires or brass rods, whichever may have been asked from the juju, piled so high as to reach far up the walls, and glinting in the early morning sunlight.

Before the treasure may be touched, magic leaves must be pounded into a fine paste and mixed with water. This medicine is called usuk, i.e. disinfectant, and should be sprinkled over the gift, to destroy all evil influences which might otherwise attach to wealth gained in so strange a way. [29] Even so, after the "first fruits" have been borne as an offering to the priest, the actual wires or rods should not be used in direct purchase of anything for the personal use of those who have wrought the spell. As soon as possible the new treasure should be exchanged for coins or produce, which can then safely be bartered for whatever is desired.

Some time ago a well-known chief of Calabar was said to have obtained considerable wealth in this fashion. He was careful to warn his wives not to enter his room, or, at any rate, to take nothing thence. One of them, however, chanced to peep within and saw a heap of money lying in one of the corners, new and shining. The temptation was too strong, so she concealed a certain sum at the bottom of her market-basket and set out.

It happened that a great catch of crayfish had been brought in by the fisher-folk that day. The sight tempted the woman, and she bought a plentiful supply, which she took home, cooked, and set before her husband. All unknowing he ate of the dish, but no sooner had the first mouthful passed his lips than he felt the juju seize him, and at once knew what had happened. He cried aloud to the woman who had served him so ill: "What have you done? You have disobeyed the word which I spoke, and now I must die for your fault." Hardly had he finished speaking when he fell down dead.

My informant is a man for whom we have the highest esteem. Strange as it may appear he believed absolutely in the truth of every word which he related. The man whose death has just been described was a great friend of his, and one of his own "age class"-- an association of those born within a few years of one another, the members of which hold together "closer than a brother." He finished his story very sadly:

"There is a man in the Kamerun to whom all such magic is known. He offered to teach my favourite brother the rites necessary in order to make him very rich. The latter came to me and said, 'If you will join with me in this business I will gladly enter upon it, but I fear to do such a thing alone.'"

To this our informant answered, "If it were now as in the old days, how gladly I would do so! As it is, I fear too much to enter upon any such thing, for to-day our wives are light of mind and unstable of heart, looking always here and there, from one man to another. Of all my wives there is none upon whom I can lean in full trust. The old order has passed away, giving place to new, and should I lay me down depending upon a wife's faithfulness, there would be but little chance of ever again awakening."

It is hard to forget the sadness of the patient voice as it uttered these words-not complainingly, but. merely as stating a fact beyond human power to remedy.

WITCHCRAFT

AS with ourselves in the Middle Ages, and, to the best of my belief, among all native tribes, there are more witches than wizards in Ibibio land; partly because there are more women than men, and should she have children a witch always passes her wicked knowledge on to one of her daughters, usually to the youngest born; partly also because it would appear easier for women to place themselves en rapport with the powers of the unseen world.

When a witch is either unwed or barren, she generally seeks out some child whom she may initiate into her secrets. For this purpose she inveigles some little one into her house and sets before it "chop" such as children love, in which "witch medicine" has been mixed. Several cases in which parents have charged suspected persons with putting witchcraft potions into their children's food were brought before my husband in the Native Courts. One such occurred just before we left Oron. The witch, a barren woman, famous for her knowledge of drugs, was accused of having administered "medicine" to a small boy in a dish of plantains mixed with palm oil. The magic having entered into him had caused him, against his will, to sally forth at night and join the unholy revels of a witch company. How such things are brought about is told in the conclusion of the story of Ekpenyong and Adiaha, the first part of which was given on pp. 89-94. It thus continues:

"Now when the enemy of Ekpenyong had consulted with the latter's discarded wife as to how the power of the guardian juju might be satisfied, she thought for a long time and then said:

"'This juju is a very strong one and would surely kill any of us who are possessed by witchcraft should we try to enter the house in order to harm those within. The safest way, therefore, is to seek to put witchcraft into one of the children. Then, when the latter has joined our company, we can send him to do our work, for the juju will not harm such a one, seeing that he is of the house. Let us therefore choose out the youngest for this service, and having invited Ekpenyong and all his family to a feast, mix witchcraft medicine with the portion of his last born.'

"To this the wicked chief agreed, and sent to beg Ekpenyong to bring Adiaha and all their children to visit his house. Now, the youngest of the family was named Offong, and for him at the feast a fine portion was set aside, in which beforehand a strong medicine had been mixed. Nothing was noticed at the time. The guests ate with enjoyment, and afterwards went home well pleased.

"A few nights later the wicked chief changed himself by evil enchantment into the form of a night bird, and flew hooting round the compound where Offong lay sleepless, for it was impossible for him to rest, because of the strange thing which had entered into him.

"'Come out,' hooted the evil bird. 'Come out, and join those who are awaiting you.'

"On this the witchcraft that was within the boy drove him forth, and to his astonishment he saw a great crowd of people before the house flitting hither and thither in the light of the moon. He cried out in surprise at sight of such a multitude, but the bad chief cautioned him never to tell anyone of what he was about to witness. Then all went together, not walking upon the ground, but floating a few feet above, until they reached a great cleared space in the bush, such as Offong had never seen before. In the midst of it was a cauldron simmering over a fire, and into this from time to time, to the lad's horror, gobbets of human flesh were thrown by one or other of the witch-company. After all had danced awhile in the light of the flame, they seated themselves in a great circle and the contents of the pot were distributed among them. To Offong was given a large piece of flesh and some yam. He ate the latter, but concealed the former, which he took home, placed in his mother's 'smoking basket,' and then hung over the fire.

"The poor boy dared not speak to anyone of what he had seen, but went in terror of his life, fearing lest any should notice the strange change that had befallen him; for, whenever the witches were playing, no matter how much lie strove to stay in the house, the witchcraft that was within him carried him through locked door or wall-chink to the meeting-place, without so much as foot set to ground.

"Every time that he was thus summoned a feast was held. and each time Offong hid his share of the human flesh as before. All through the night they danced, from nightfall to cock-crow, but just before dawn-break the unhappy boy always found himself once more safe in bed. By day he went in terror among his own kin; for, whenever Ekpenyong called his family together to make sacrifice before the juju which protected the household from evil powers, Offong feared that the spirit would catch him on account of the witchcraft that was within him. When, therefore, the others crowded round to join in the sacrifice, he kept to the outskirts of the circle, trembling lest what had befallen him should be revealed.

"Thus many moons passed, till at length one night the wicked chief said that it was now Offong's turn to provide a man for the feast. Shaking with terror the boy pleaded that he was too young to have men at his disposal, and that, indeed, he had no one to give.

"On this the evil beings rose gibbering around him, and with harsh voices and menacing hands cried that he must bring father, mother, brother or sister for them to devour; else, should he fail to do so, they would rend him in pieces and fling him into the pot.

"Offong knew not to whom to turn in his trouble, but at length decided to tell all to Akpan, his eldest brother, by whose side he slept at night. To him, therefore, amid bitter tears, he confided how he had been drawn into the witch-company against his will, and forced to attend meetings where human beings were devoured, although up till that time no morsel of the accursed food had passed his own lips.

At first Akpan could not believe so strange a tale, but Offong went out and brought in proof the meat which he had con-cealed and preserved in his mother's drying basket. When the elder brother had examined this he could no longer doubt, but comforted the boy as best he could, bidding him seem to consent to the demand of those evil beings, and plead for a few days' grace in which to provide a victim. Then he himself went out to a lonely place in the bush and sat down to consider the matter. After thinking for awhile he decided to seek out the juju man to whom his father had gone before his own birth. At once he set forth, and after marching for many miles reached the dwelling of this wise adviser. After laying the whole trouble before him, the suppliant was given a medicine so strong that no evil thing could withstand its power.

"Armed with this, Akpan returned home and bade Offong go to the head of his witch-company and say that he was now ready to sacrifice his elder brother, but, as he himself was too small to carry so heavy a body to the meeting-place, he begged that the chief himself would come at the head of the witch folk to bear it away. To this all gladly consented, suspecting nothing.

"Then Akpan strewed the strong medicine upon the ground and made sacrifice to the guardian juju, by which its power was increased, so that when at nightfall the evil creatures gathered round the compound, the charm held them and they could not flee away.

"At break of dawn the lads woke their father and bade him come forth with all his family. There, before the house, the witches were found naked and trembling. No sooner did these perceive that their evil nature could no longer be hid than they started screaming like bats and ill birds of night, running round and round seeking a hiding-place, yet could not escape because the juju held them. Then Ekpenyong beat upon the great drum, and summoned all the townsfolk together, and they bound those evil creatures, both witches and wizards, and dragged them forth to the juju house. There they sat in judgment and pronounced sentence that all the witch company should be burnt to death save their chief alone. Him they bound to a tree, and, while still alive, tore small pieces from his body, which they roasted before his eyes, then forced him to eat, crying:

"'Because he was more evil than all the others and has devoured the flesh of many innocent people, now he shall eat his own meat!'

"After awhile he also died in great agony. Since that day the townsfolk have shunned the spot, for in the tree to which he was bound night birds have made their nests and may often be heard hooting and crying through the darkness with ill-boding voices."

Many witchcraft rites are carried out by jealous fellow-wives, and especially by barren women in order to steal away the babe which a rival is about to bear. The means to this end are carefully guarded secrets, but several such cases were related to me by women informants, and the following may perhaps be quoted as typical:

"A barren wife says to herself, 'Why should I have this pain at my heart because our husband gives his love and his gifts to another woman! Why have I no piccan to hold in my arms while this other has already borne a babe and is about to bear again?

"Then the unhappy woman goes to a powerful witch-doctor, usually some ancient crone who has grown old in the study of secret things such as these. There she buys a strong medicine, and at night-time enters into the room where her happy rival sleeps by the side of their common husband. By magic arts she draws out the 'dream body' of the piccan, and bears it off to the bush, where a company of witches, brought thither by the witch-doctor, are waiting to devour it. Witches by their magic can feed upon the essence of things, leaving the tangible forms apparently unaltered. Next morning the babe lies dead within the womb, because it has no soul. Then the mother begins to cry 'Who killed my piccan? The barren woman sits in her house laughing low to herself, and her rival hears her laughter.

"After the small dead body has been laid in the ground beneath the earthen bowl which custom has decreed for such burials, the bereaved woman goes in her turn to a juju man and asks

'Who killed my piccan?' He is almost sure to know the circumstances, and usually answers, 'If a barren woman dwells in your house she it is who stole your babe's dream shape to devour so that the child died.'

"Then the mother comes home and goes round the compound perpetually wailing, 'Who killed my piccan? Let whosoever did this come before me!'

No one answers. So she walks up and down, to and fro, before the door of her rival, continually calling, 'Who killed my piccan?' At length the witch-wife grows weary of the constant repetition, and asks, 'You speak to me?' Whereon the mother, pointing against her an accusing arm, replies, 'You killed my piccan!'

"Whenever they meet the accusation is repeated until at length the witch-wife can bear it no more, so she takes money and goes to the Native Court, or before the chiefs, saying, 'Stop this woman from asking about the death of her babe.' Whereon they answer, 'If you are guiltless, why should you try to prevent her from crying?' Often a husband thus learns who it is who has killed his unborn child, and casts out the barren woman from his house."

One evening just as dusk was falling, one of my women informants began of her own accord, to speak of the belief in a ghoul, or elemental, whose principal object it is to destroy babes in the womb. She spoke in a low, nervous voice, glancing furtively every now and then over her shoulder into the deepening shadows, as though she feared that some evil thing might be lurking within them, ready to spring forth and punish her for revealing so dread a secret. To quote her words:

"There is a kind of devil which never sleeps at night time nor is seen by day. In the depths of the bush or in waste places he may be met gleaming from out the darkness with a pale light, but should one see him it is best to flee away lest one die of terror.

"At first he seems no taller than a man, but after awhile he swells and grows very big, as if made of smoke which rises higher and higher, and through which at times flames can be seen to gleam. I myself once saw such a one in the bush near Ndiya. There was a light amid the trees and I asked my companion, 'What is that?' But he answered, 'Let us run. It is the evil thing seeking unborn babes.' So we fled.

"After the smoke body has grown so high and broad that it reaches even to the tops of the great cotton trees, the spirit can condense at will till it becomes so small that it can creep through the narrowest door-cranny or wall-chink.

"When a woman lies sleeping with a babe near birth beneath her heart, this devil enters softly, softly, in the night time when all is very still. He draws from her that which was within, and bears it into the depths of the bush to devour in part, and partly to make a strong medicine from which his evil power is obtained.

"The woman sleeps on and knows nothing of the loss which has befallen her, but when she wakes at dawn pain rends her. Afterwards she finds out her misfortune, so her heart is very sore."

At Ikotobo some time ago a man died under strong suspicion of having perished as the result of a spell wrought by a woman of the same town. The dead man's friends sallied forth and captured the supposed witch. They bound her by strong ropes round wrists and ankles, then bore her forth to a place in the bush where there is a deep gully, shouting at intervals, "Abassi will punish you for what you have done! You are going to die to-day!"

When the top of the bank from which they meant to throw their captive was reached, they made her call upon the name of Abassi, saying, "If I killed the man of whose death I am accused, may I die also! If I did not do so, may Abassi save me!"

After this, bound and helpless as she was, they flung the woman down the steep bank, watching till the bush closed over and hid her from sight. Then all went home again, saying that they had rid their town of an evil thing. Next morning, however, as they went on their way to farm work, lo! the same woman was seen going quietly about her house as if nothing had happened.

Then all the people rejoiced, saying, "This was no witch. She is cleared from all guilt. Abassi has helped her, as she prayed, therefore she is proved blameless."

Here, as in most parts of the world, the task of weaving evil spells is greatly simplified to witch and wizard if something closely connected with the intended victim can be secured. Such things are laid before the shrine of some bad juju, while prayer is made that the spirit will follow the trail of him to whom the relic belongs and destroy him utterly.

This course was much resorted to in the old days to prevent the escape of slaves, for many who would have run the risk of capture by their earthly masters dared not face the dread of being "caught" by the juju, upon whose shrine a lock of hair, nail parings, or a rag from a long-worn cloth had been laid as an aid to possible tracking.

An excellent example of the power attributed to such things is given in Dr. Haddon's "Magic and Fetishism":

"The potency of the hair," he says, "is shown beaded band in the beliefs about the long, narrow which is used to tie up the hair of a Musquakie woman. This, though a talisman when first worn, becomes something infinitely more sacred and precious, being transfused with the essence of her soul; anyone gaining possession of it has her for an abject slave if he keeps it, and kills her if he destroys it. A woman will go from a man she loves to a man she hates if he has contrived to possess himself of her hair string; and a man will forsake wife and children for a witch who has touched his lips with her hair string. The hair string is made for a girl by her mother or grandmother, and decorated with a 'luck pattern,' it is also prayed over by the maker and a Shaman."

An almost identical belief clings round the long, plaited bags which we found among the women of the Banana tribe on the Logone river, in French Central Africa. For each girl babe one such is woven by her mother or grandmother, and with it her life's thread is thought to be mysteriously linked. No bribe would induce a living woman to part with one, since with its departure her soul must leave her, but we were fortunate enough to purchase several which had belonged to dead members of the tribe.

A curious superstition concerning rags as an instrument of witchcraft was confided to me by an Ibibio woman, on the usual pledge that under no circumstances should her name be disclosed, for this also is among the women's mysteries which no man may learn.

"When one of us hates a rival very bitterly," said my informant, "she desires above all things either to take the life of her enemy or render her barren. One of the surest ways of bringing this about is to touch the body of the intended victim with a piece from an old cloth long worn by one now dead, or if that should be found impossible, to lay some fragment of such a cloth among the garments or utensils used by the woman whom it is sought to injure, or to bury it just beneath the surface in some spot over which she is sure to tread."

A kindred belief as to the power of such rags to inflict the curse of sterility is recorded from our own northern climes. To quote Dr. Haddon, "In Germany and Denmark . . . to hang rags from the clothing of a dead man upon a vine is to render it barren." [30]

Such beliefs are hardly to be wondered at when one considers that the dread of witchcraft is still so powerful in out of the way parts of the British Isles, that people suspected of having entered into league with the powers of evil are even now occasionally done to death. Comparatively recently, too, Father Praniatis, the "expert" called in to give evidence in court during the Beiliss trial at Kieff, calmly stated "That there was perhaps more witchcraft in the twentieth century than there had been in the Middle Ages."

Many superstitions which show a strong family likeness to those of the West Coast of Africa are still rife among us. In 1913, for instance, a verdict of manslaughter was returned at the Ulster Assizes against a man named Thomas Flynn, who had been charged with the murder of John Prior near Ballyconnell, County Cavan. Upon the neck of the corpse were found two gashes inflicted after death, in consequence of the superstition that were such wounds made upon the body of a man killed by accident, his ghost would not be able to return to plague those responsible for his death.

Among the Ibibios, also, elaborate precautions are taken to prevent the return of ghosts. Before burial the bodies of those suspected of witchcraft have nose, mouth, eyes and ears filled with native pitch extracted from a cactus thought to be an object of dread to beings possessed by evil powers.

More particularly do widows who have been consoled for the loss of their husbands, or such as had wished to be freed from the marriage yoke, fear the return of the shades of former spouses.

"Young men cut off before their time," so one of my women informants explained, "are often forced to leave their 'best wife' behind." To quote her words, spoken in quaint, halting English:

"The dead husband loved his wife so kind that he did not want to leave her in this world, since without her he was very lonely among the ghosts. So he strove to kill her that she might follow him to Obio Ekkpo," i.e. the Ghost Town.

When the thoughts of a widow have already turned to another wooer she is terrified lest the spirit of her former husband should return and seek to draw her after him to the ghost realm. Should she have reason to suppose that such is the case, she goes to an Idiong man who has a great reputation for second sight. By his advice, "chop" is cooked and placed in one comer of her room. The priest takes up a position immediately before this, and stands calling upon the name of the ghost. Close to the place where the food is laid some member of the family crouches, holding a strong pot, preferably of iron, tilted forward ready to invert over the one in which the food is served. When the Idiong man makes a sign that the ghost is busy eating, and that, in enjoyment of the feast, the latter has temporarily forgotten to look after his safety, the second pot is clapped over the first, and both are then bound firmly together, thus keeping the spirit imprisoned between.

If, on the contrary, a widow loved her husband very much, she will cook "chop" for him after his death and place it secretly in a comer of her room so that his spirit may be induced to return and enjoy it.

JUJUS

OF jujus there are two kinds, good and bad. The former are usually termed idemm by Ibibios and ndemm by Efiks, while the latter are called mbiam. By a queer turn of native thought all, or nearly all--for in spite of careful inquiry many details were probably concealed from us--idemms would appear to have female attributes, and most of these beneficent jujus bear the additional title "Bestower of Babes"; yet no authenticated example of an idemm priestess has reached our cars. The cult would appear to be served only by men. Of mbiam priestesses, on the other hand, the names of several could be given, though it is better not to do so, since the greater number of these appear as far as possible to seek to conceal their identity from the males of the tribe. To them, however, go women in trouble, especially those who wish to invoke the aid of the juju to remove a successful rival from their path, or inflict the curse of barrenness upon a more favoured fellow wife. Such a case came before the Native Court when a woman, Unang Obo by name, accused one Teahri of invoking mbiam against her. In the course of the evidence Ese Efiom, sworn, stated.

I am an mbiam priestess. The defendant never came to me to ask me to invoke mbiam on Unang Obo. The accused and other women came to the juju house and took an mbiam drum to beat round the town, calling people to assemble and give reason why a calabash was broken."

This last-mentioned action was usually taken by a wife who wished to divorce herself from her husband on the ground that he was keeping a woman who had already borne twins as wife or sweetheart. A calabash, or native pot, is always regarded as the feminine symbol, as is a spear that of the opposite sex. To break a calabash, therefore, signifies that a woman no longer regards herself as the wife of the man to whom she has hitherto been married.

Another example of this custom came before the Native Court at Ikotobo, in which the plaintiff stated:

"Defendant is my husband. I had no son. After he married me one of his wives took an empty calabash and ran round the market beating it with her hands, and shouting, 'My husband has married this woman, therefore I have nothing more to do with him.' By our custom, if the old wives were not satisfied with a new one whom their husband brought to the house, they used to proclaim publicly, 'My husband has married such a woman. I will have nothing more to do with him'--knocking at the same time upon the calabash. As she beat it she cried, 'The new wife has already borne twins,' after which she went away. Last year, however, she came back and was his wife once more. On that I told defendant to divorce me, but he replied, 'I cannot do so.' Some time later he wished to become a member of the Idiong society, and I helped him to gather together the entrance money, but after the ceremonies were over he said, I can no longer be your husband.'

"Then, on account of the money which I had given him, I refused to go away, but he said, 'I am now a member of Idiong, and if you do not leave me Idiong himself will kill you.' At that time there were several Court Messengers present. I said, 'First you must pay me back what I gave to help you join this society'; but my husband said, 'You must keep yourself for the future, for if you do not go away from me you will certainly die.'

"In revenge for this treatment the woman went to an mbiam priestess and bought a bottle of juju medicine, which she buried in the yard, believing that this would bring about the death of her husband and that of her rival."

Beside its functions as giver of babes and bestower of prosperity on farm and byre, an idemm juju is thought to exercise a beneficent influence not only upon its worshippers, but even upon their descendants to the third and fourth generation, should such be reduced to poverty.

A story illustrating this gentler aspect of juju worship is told of a man named Akpan Adia Agbo, of Ikot Akpan, who died some fifteen years ago. While yet a small boy he had the misfortune to lose both his parents, first his father and then his mother, and was left with nothing to eat and none to care for him. When he went round to the houses of the townsfolk they drove him away, so he crept off by himself and slept in the Egbo shed. At dawn each day he left his sleeping-place lest he should be driven forth, and went out searching for something to eat.

When he came to the place where the juju offerings were laid before the shrine, sometimes a small chicken, and sometimes a few plantains were to be found.

Now his parents had been pious people who had always given of their best to the juju. Before the mother died she had gathered together all that she had and offered it as a last sacrifice, praying that the spirit might protect her son and be to him as a mother, since there was none other to care for him.

So the boy took what he found and ate fearlessly, cooking the food in a secret place, and trusting that the juju would do him no harm for the theft.

For several years he lived thus, but at length a sister of his dead father, who some years before had married and gone to a distant town, came back, and finding the boy deserted, took him to her home. There she fed him well, and showed him every kindness, but when he was grown up the longing came to go back to his own people. So the woman said, "Very well, if you are able to feed yourself you can go:"

On reaching his native town the lad asked to be shown the place where his father's mimbo farm was. When the people saw how big and strong he had grown they agreed to do as he wished, and led him thither.

At once he began to cut mimbo, and they found that his palm trees bore sap more plentifully than those of all the other townsfolk. He sold the wine for a good price, and with the money bought goats and sheep. These latter bore kids and lambs in great abundance, so that he soon grew rich and was able to marry a wife strong and tall, who bore him many piccans.

Whatever he undertook succeeded, so that those who had driven him forth as a boy began to come under him, and in the end he became head chief of Ikot Akpan. In his house dwelt threescore wives, and sons and daughters so numerous that he never counted them. All this prosperity came to him because the juju helped him, and blessed everything that he did from the time when he was lonely and deserted and had no sustenance save that which he took from the sacrifices.

A very different story, embodying the attributes more usually connected with the idea of juju worship, was told us by Idaw Imuk, half-brother of the head chief and most famous juju priest of the town where the events are said to have taken place. It may perhaps be called:

AN IBOIBO IPHIGENIA.

In the old days there was a very famous juju at Idua Eket. The name of this was Edogho Idua, and it was the dominant juju for many miles round.

"Only a little time before Government came to our country, one of the principal chiefs of Idua, Ukpon by name, wanted to join the cult, for the spirit was said to be strong to protect, and rich to bestow blessings upon its worshippers, as well as swift to avenge wrongs done them by enemies. In preparation for the initiatory feast many goats were brought, cows also, with yams and plantains innumerable; palm wine too and all that is necessary to make glad the hearts of guests. So soon as everything was in readiness Ukpon sent round to all the countryside to bid the people come and rejoice with him over his entry into the cult.

"In great numbers they came and ate up all the good things provided for their entertainment. Seven days they feasted, playing the play of the juju, and dancing and singing continuously both by day and night. When some of the dancers grew weary and went to rest, others took their places, so that the sound of rejoicing rose ceaselessly in the cars of the juju during all that time.

"On the eighth day they left off dancing and gathered round to witness the last and greatest sacrifice. A man who had been bought for the purpose was led forth and slain before the shrine. As the blood of the victim bespattered the fetish, Ukpon cried out boastfully, 'See, Edogho! This is but a dog! If you protect me well I will bring you far better offerings!'

"At once the juju answered, 'So ho! It is but a dog which you have sacrificed to me. If you do not at once therefore fetch me a man I will not help you at all.'

"On hearing this Ukpon repented of his boastfulness and was very sorry, for he had not counted upon the extra expense of a second offering; but the wrath of the juju was too terrible to be braved, so he went forth obediently and bought another victim, thinking that Edogho would be satisfied at last.

"To his grief, however, the juju announced, 'Because of the word you have spoken you must bring me a human sacrifice every year for seven years, and the one which I choose first of all is your first-born piccan.'

"To this Ukpon answered, 'Rather than sacrifice the little daughter who is my only child I will forfeit all the gifts which have already been spent upon you and leave your cult to-day'; but the juju answered:

"'Not so. If you leave me I will destroy the whole town this very night.'

"On hearing this cruel saying Ukpon turned round and called upon the townsfolk, crying:

"'The juju asks for my only child. I beg you, therefore, help me to collect the other sacrifices which he demands, so that this dear one may be spared.'

"On hearing this the people consulted together, and at length arranged that seven compounds should, each in turn, provide a man every year, till the seven years were over.

"Thus they did, but after that time was up they came to Ukpon and said, 'We are not able to pay this toll any more. For a long time now we have given a man each year, but now we can do so no more.'

"So Ukpon went before the priest and put the case to him, begging that his foolish speech might be forgotten, and that all might now be well. Through the mouth of his servant, however, the spirit made answer:

"'You called upon the townsfolk to help you, but in vain. In spite of all that you have done I will take your piccan in my own way.'

"Now in the meantime the girl had grown up to be a maiden so beautiful that she was sought in marriage by many youths. She was still the only child of her house and the pride of both her parents. Yet, knowing that it was useless to struggle further, when the time came round for the annual sacrifice Ukpon led her before the Juju.

"Bitterly the girl wept as she went to the shrine, and bitterly wept the mother, but it was all of no avail. Her young blood gushed forth and the reek of it was sweet in the nostrils of Edogho Idua.

"In despair at the sight of his pitiful dead, Ukpon cried out, 'If I had only known the ways of this juju I would never have had anything to do with it! Should the juju keep on like this I will take it and throw it into the water!'

"Then the spirit announced in a terrible voice, through the mouth of the priest his servant, 'Before you throw me into the water I will destroy you utterly with all your house.'

"That night the compound of the unfortunate man burst into flame, and himself, his wife and all within were utterly consumed.

"After that the other townsfolk feared 'too much' to place themselves in the power of so terrible a juju. No fresh members joined the cult. It lost its power, and since Government came to our country, it has had no more authority within the town."

Chief Ansa Ekang Ita Henshaw told us of a place called Eise, which, according to his account, lies opposite to Akuna-Akuna on the Cross River. Here there is said to be a very powerful crocodile juju, in connection with which is a priestess. There appears to be no mystery about the celebration of the rites of this cult. Anyone, so we were told, either white or black, may witness them, which is fortunate, since otherwise it would be difficult to believe that Chief Ansa's story was of actual present-day happenings, rather than a page torn from some as yet unpublished novel by Sir H. Rider Haggard.

Coming across this tale in a place so reminiscent of scenes through which in the days of our youth we hurried breathless, led by the author's magic, the thought forced itself upon us as to the ingratitude with which we regard many writers who, all unknown to us, had so great an influence in determining the course of our lives. To the great authors of old we are forced to yield some tithe of their due, because they have marked us so deeply with their mark that we see to a certain extent at least through their eyes, and even when coming suddenly upon a scene of surpassing beauty find ourselves repeating their very words, because none other seem fitted to describe it. We could not forget them if we would, for from Homer and his great brothers of song, from Virgil, Herodotus, and many a less-known Roman and Greek, sayings, forgotten till the moment, suddenly come to mind at some fresh sight as if spoken anew in one's ear. So it is too with Beowulf and the Maldon Poem, with the sweet haunting rhymes of old ballads and the great moderns: Dante, Shakespeare, Goethe, Keats, and Shelley--all demand a gratitude which we could not withhold if we would; but as for men of the present day--to how many of these do we offer adequate tribute for having first turned our thoughts to adventure or research, to the glory of man's work on the edges of Empire, to the fascination of seeking for old-world treasures, hidden in forgotten glades and amid long-buried cities, or the joy of penetrating secrets behind the back of beyond?

With something of all this in mind we accepted the offer of one of our kind friends at Oron to take with us on a six hours' canoe journey a copy of "The Yellow God."

In a country where every tree and stone hides a story which is simply crying out to be written down, it seemed almost wrong to give any time at all to the reading of one safely printed; but the temptation to see how a writer, who to one's youthful fancy seemed to breathe the very essence of Africa--the terrible and mysterious--would stand the hard test of reading in an open canoe, amid scenes so near to those which he describes, was irresistible. The accuracy of description and the convincingly real language of the wonderful Jeekie came as a surprise. It was pleasant to slip back again into the atmosphere of childhood, even at the cost of finding a description of the fall of one of the great trees, witnessed by us a little while before, given almost word for word as we had written it down on reaching camp some half hour after the occurrence. A pencil stump soon erased the passage from our manuscript, and a few days later

Chief Ansa's story was told us. It is given as nearly as possible in the words of my informant.

"To the left of the town of Eise lies a river in which live crocodiles of many kinds--big, mighty ones, and others very small. The people honour these as their juju, and of this cult a woman is always chosen to be the head. When the priestess grows too old to serve fittingly any more, the King Crocodile himself chooses out a new one. The way in which the choice is made is as follows:

"In the night-time the lord of all the crocodiles goes himself or sends a messenger into the town. Through the quiet streets the great reptile creeps, straight for the house of the woman who has been chosen. Arrived there he lays him down by the wall behind which glow the 'seeds of fire' kept alive for the cooking of the morrow's meal.

"When people come forth at dawn they see the great beast lying before the house, and know at once the meaning of the sight. Where there is but one woman in the family she is forthwith acclaimed as the new priestess; but as this is hardly ever the case, the townsfolk go round and try to find out which of the women in the house is the one chosen for the service. All are led before the diviner, and trial made of each in turn, until one is named for the honour.

"When this has happened the old priestess knows that her time has come, for it is the will of the lord crocodile that she should die. Uncomplainingly, therefore, she hands over everything to her successor, teaches her all the lore of the cult which has been handed down to herself from a long line of predecessors, and, when all is ended, quietly lies down never again to rise.

"Whenever anyone in the town has offended against the law of the juju, a sign is given so that the evil-doer may be sought out and punished. So sure as the chief crocodile is angered he sends forth one of his breed as a messenger, who goes up into the town and catches a dog in his jaws. This he carries to the water, and then swims up and down with his prey held aloft, so that all the people may see and take notice.

"Then the townsfolk know that one of their number has transgressed against the law of the juju, and that, because of this, trouble is about to fall upon them. So they consult the oracle, and try to find out which is the sinner, and begin to get together a sacrifice in order to appease the wrath of the sacred reptiles.

"Only the priestess may offer sacrifice. At the edge of the water she stands, calling upon the name of the juju, a live chicken held aloft in her hand. After awhile one of the holy crocodiles is seen swimming slowly towards her. He lays his head on the bank by her feet, waiting until the prayer is finished, after which she bends down and sets the chicken close by his cruel jaws. Sometimes he swallows it at once, sometimes lets it run a little way, then dashes after, but always catches it in the end, and dives with it beneath the water. Next, rum or palm wine is poured into a horn or into one of the long cucumber-shaped calabashes. The priestess chants a new invocation and the beast comes to the surface again. Then she cries aloud, 'Behold! I bring you your drink offering,' at which he opens his mouth and receives the libation. After that he waits until the last rite is over, on which land-dwellers and water-dwellers alike all go back to their homes.

"One of the strangest things about this strange cult is that the crocodile is said never to accept any chicken which has once been owned by a 'twin mother.' No matter how cunningly people may seek to deceive him in the matter by passing the bird through many hands, or however long a time it may have been kept in other compounds, should it ever have been in the possession of a 'twin woman' the crocodile will know this and refuse to appear at the call of the priestess to receive the polluted offering.

"On great occasions a ram or goat is sacrificed. This is too heavy for the priestess to hold up by herself alone, so two men usually help her, standing one on either hand.

"So soon as her cry is heard ringing out from beneath the uplifted ram, nine crocodiles are said to be seen hastening down stream. In the midst of them swims their chief, the King Crocodile, a big mighty beast, very old, with the others stretching out, four on either side, as if to guard him. Straight to the feet of the priestess swims the central figure, while the rest stay a little way off. Then the ram-bearers step to the edge of the water into which they fling their burden. This the great reptile seizes in his jaws and drags under, while his eight companions dive beneath the surface in order to share the sacrifice with him.

"Such were the rites of this juju ordained to our fathers before the great trees of the forest were yet formed as small seeds in the heart of the flowers which bore them, and such are the rites which last unchanged till to-day."

This account is quite unconfirmed, but we hope some day to visit Eise and make the acquaintance of its priestess.

WOMAN AND SECRET SOCIETIES

THERE are still one or two secret societies among Ibibio women, though none so powerful as the great Ekoi cult of Nimm, or the famous Bundu of Sierra Leone. One of these is Ebere, a play which was started among the Ubium Ibibios, but was thought so beautiful that it was copied by other tribes. The principal rule of this society concerns the dress of the members, which is rather costly, so that only the wealthy are able to join. A large number of silk handkerchiefs must be bought and pleated. The corners are gathered together in a rosette and knotted along the ceinture so as to overlap slightly, while the lower end floats free. Bands of tanned skin, three to four inches broad, are then cut, and on these cowries and coloured beads are so thickly sewn as almost to hide the foundation. Two such bands are bound on each leg, usually above the ankle and below the knee. Sometimes a like adornment is worn on each of the forearms, while round the firm brown throats and over the breasts hang chains of bright-hued beads. Beneath the ankle-band hang dozens of the little twisted brass ornaments called nyawhawraw, such as are worn by small girls in front from a string round the waist. These ornaments are sometimes spoken of as "bells," but they are really more like little clappers. Ebere women say that they wear them round their ankles, "so that they should clash together and sing sweetly in the dance."

Such associations strike a note midway between Freemasonry and Trade Unionism, and form the only safeguard of Ibibio women against the tyranny of their men-folk. Should a member consider herself wronged the matter is laid before the heads of the society, and action taken according to their decision.

Not long ago a ease was brought before the Native Court at Idua Oron, in which a woman, Nse Abassi by name, took action against Odiong Ete, as representative of the local Ebere Society, for unlawfully demanding money from her.

The plaintiff stated on oath

"Accused came to my house accompanied by Eyo Inyan and also Eurpe and Atati. With them they bore the Ebere drum, and when they came in they sat down and placed it upon the table. They said they were going to fine me one goat and one demijohn of rum because my goats had spoiled Nteyo's farm. I gave them one small demi-john and two small bottles of rum on the first day. Four days later I bought a goat and paid it over to the accused, also another demi-john."

Nku Ita, called as witness, stated on oath:

"I was not present when the accused demanded the goat and rum, but plaintiff came to me and bought rum, saying that it was to pay a fine inflicted by accused as head of the Ebere Society."

In every town both among Efiks and other Ibibios there is a branch of the Than Isong Society, i.e. the Women of the Land. For the rites of this cult members gather together at certain times of the year, and not one man may be present. At Calabar it is called Ndito Iban, and it is in connection with this that warriors' wives dress in male attire and go about gaily dancing and singing, while their men-folk are on the war path.

The rites would seem to bear some faint, far-off echo of those of the Alruna wives who, with locks arranged beard-like, prayed All-Father Odin from over the Swans' Bath to bless their men's arms.

The Pangwe woman's secret society, Mawungu, also shows points of resemblance with the Ibibio Than Isong. Not only is the dance with which the festivities close called "Eban," according to Herr Gunter Tessmann, but the performers dress in male attire, while their leader marches gun in hand and sword girded.

As night fell on the day when Efik warriors left the town, the wives who remained behind used to go to their sleeping-rooms and there don the garments of their absent lords. With his clothing the head wife also took the name of her husband, and while the ceremony lasted might call herself, or be addressed, by no other. Once clad in this strange attire, the women sallied forth to visit the chief compounds of the town, drinking palm wine, laughing and jesting at each. No matter how heavy and anxious might be the hearts beneath this manly guise, they dared not show the least sign of sadness or anxiety, but must appear happy and brave, that by sympathetic magic the courage of their absent husbands should be upheld.

The ceremony was called "Ikom Be," and it was most strictly forbidden that any man should witness it; for this also was among the women's mysteries, and destruction would have fallen upon the race should any male have profaned the rites by his presence. All night long the women danced round the town to prove their courage and endurance. Only after dawn-break might they creep back to rest, and even then tears were forbidden lest indulgence in such weakness might magically affect their absent lords--turning to water the hearts within their breasts and causing their strength to melt away.

Somewhat similar precautions are recorded from Borneo, where "When men are on a war expedition, fires are lighted at home, the mats are spread, and the fires kept up till late in the evening and lighted again before dawn so that the men may not be cold; the roofing of the house is opened before dawn so that the man may not lie too long and so fall into the enemy's hands. Again when a Dyak is out headhunting his wife, or, if he is unmarried, his sister, must wear a sword day and night in order that he may be always thinking of his weapons; and she may not sleep during the day nor go to bed before two in the morning lest her husband or brother should thereby be surprised in his sleep by an enemy." [31]

As an example of the way in which native customs are some-times misunderstood by even the best-meaning of white men, it may perhaps be mentioned that a missionary of great expe-rience and high standing on the West Coast who had heard something of the Efik rites above described, related them in somewhat garbled form as proof of the joy of these women on being temporarily released from the control of their men-folk!

Although these two societies, Ebere and Than Isong, are the only ones which we were able to trace as still existing among Ibibio women, yet accident brought to light a very different state of affairs which had obtained in former days.

While collecting information concerning the ceremonies which custom had decreed should be performed on the deaths of Efik chiefs who had held great positions in the Egbo Society--the most important secret cult among Efik and Ekoi men--my husband discovered that when "the Egbo" flees the town, as he is usually supposed to do after such an event, should the surviving members fail to catch and bring him back in triumph, they are forced to enlist the services of an ancient woman who must belong to one of the ruling families. At her call the spirit usually returns, although he has refused to pay attention to the summons of any man. This need to ask the help of a woman seemed strange in a society from which women are excluded on penalty of death from witnessing the rites. My husband therefore inquired as to the origin of the custom and was told, after considerable hesitation, that feminine aid was necessary because Egbo was originally a woman's secret society, until the men wrested from them its secrets, learnt the rites, and then drove out women from all participation therein. [32]

To-day, save in the depths of the bush, where many of the old ceremonies are still carried out whenever there seems a chance of eluding the vigilance of "Government," death can no longer be inflicted on women who have trespassed, either accidentally or with intention, on places set apart for the carrying out of Egbo plays. One such execution, however, happened just before our arrival at Oban, and is thus described:

"The sacred images, etc. are carried to a part of the bush where a little hut of green boughs has been built to receive them. Sentries are posted to keep all intruders from coming within a mile of this spot. On one occasion, however, two young girls, sisters, happened to have missed the patrol and trespassed unwittingly within the sacred precincts, probably in search of nuts or bush fruits which abound everywhere. They were caught by the sentries, brought before the Egbo, condemned to death and hanged almost immediately. Their brother, who was a member of the highest grade of the society, was allowed as a great favour to be present at their death, and afterwards to carry home the bodies to his family. Of redress in such a case there could be neither hope nor thought." [33]

Later we learned that the original discoverers of Egbo were some women of the Kamerun who went at dawn one morning to fish in the river. There, by the waterside, they found the first Egbo which had been brought thither by a divine woman who had come down to earth on purpose to teach the secrets of the cult to her human sisters. After learning the mysteries the women bore the image in triumph to their town, where they built a hut in which to shelter it and practise the rites of the cult. After awhile the men noticed the importance of the new institution and persuaded the women to admit them to its mysteries. No sooner had they succeeded in learning these than they rose and slew all those to whom the secret had first been revealed, and made a law that for the future only men might become members of the society or be permitted to witness the rites.

A vivid account of the death of a woman who peeped at Egbo is given by the Rev. Hope Waddell:

"Making her sit on the ground," he says, "they danced round her, leapt and capered hither and thither, ringing their bells, beating their drums and flourishing their swords over her head, or, occasionally as they passed, touching the back of her neck with the cold edge to make her shrink and shudder. At length, at a signal, the fatal stroke was given."

Such was the "justice" meted out by the usurping male to women who dared intrude upon the secrets of a cult the mysteries of which had once been exclusively their own.

That the most dreaded of all Ibibio secret societies, Ekkpo Njawhaw, i.e. Ghosts--The Destroyers, [34] was originally also a woman's society is proved by the following story compiled from three accounts, only varying slightly in detail, which were collected from different parts of the District.

How Men Stole the Secrets of the Woman's Society Ekkpo Njawhaw

In the old, old days Ibibio women were more powerful than the men, for to them alone the mysteries of the gods and of secret things were made known. By such knowledge they were enabled to keep all males as servants, employing them to do the heaviest work. Especially because of the strength of their limbs and greater endurance were men found useful as fighters.

Now at first women greatly outnumbered men upon earth, but after awhile the latter began to multiply, and in course of time grew discontented with their lot. "Why," asked they, "should the hardest work fall to our share, while the women lord it over us? Yet, body for body, they are weaker than we!" To this others answered, "So long as the secret knowledge is theirs alone, we shall never prevail against them." Thus the men whispered together, striving to find a way by which they might cast off the women's yoke.

Then, on a day very long ago, the people of Oduko went out to fight those of Urua Eye, whom after a hard struggle they overcame and drove forth into the bush. The victors began to burn down the town, but in a house built for the meeting-place of one of the women's secret societies they found abandoned strange masks and fetishes, together with fringed robes and all else necessary for carrying out the rites of the terrible cult Ekkpo Njawhaw (Ghosts--The Destroyers). These things the warriors bore back to their town, and showed to the old men who, by our custom, always stay at home during war time. Long they consulted together as to the meaning of the things and of their hidden powers. Yet, of all that they wished to know they could guess nothing. Then one very wise old man said:

"Let us get together an offering of goats and palm wine and take it before the women, begging them to teach us the mysteries that we also may know them and grow strong."

To this all agreed, and a great feast was made. Then, after they had eaten and drunken together, that old man, the wily one, went apart with some of the elder women such as were leaders among them, and spoke cunningly to these saying:

"Better to tell us the reason of Ekkpo Njawhaw, and teach us the rites of the cult, because all the men of this town want to join with the women in the matter, that together our people may become strong beyond all others."

Then the head priestess said to another old woman of Oduko:

"Let us draw apart from the men so that the women can consult alone and in secret upon the matter. It seems to me that much whispering should take place behind closed doors or in the hidden parts of the bush, for soft and slow should our steps fall upon this new road by which the men seek to lead us."

To this the second old woman answered:

"As for me, I am against it altogether. I do not want to teach our mysteries to the men, for I think that they are trying to deceive us, and wish to take Ekkpo Njawhaw away from us so that we should not be able to rule them any more."

Then these two wise ones spoke to the younger women and said: "We will give the men no part in our society." But the others cried out upon them, saying that they were foolish and over slow, caring only for the things of yesterday and taking no thought for the morrow. In the end the younger women announced:

"It is good that the men should know these things. Are they not our own men, who have always served us? Why, therefore, should we keep the secrets hidden from them?"

So with loud and eager talk they beat down the advice of the old ones who would have stayed them, until the latter said:

"Be it as you will, since you do not choose to listen, we say no more. Nevertheless we know that when the men have learnt the secrets they will take Ekkpo Njawhaw away from us so that we can never rule them as before."

Then the younger women explained to the men all the mysteries of the cult, with the full rites and every secret by means of which they had formerly held dominion. Afterwards the men called a great meeting and announced:

"From now on a law is made that should any woman try to join in the play of Ekkpo Njawhaw, the men will lead her to the market-place and there cut off her head in the sight of all the people."

On hearing this the women were very sorry for what they had done, but they dared not disobey, because the men were stronger of limb than they and also very cruel. Only the two old women who had not agreed to tell the secrets said:

"We were never willing to open up these mysteries to the men, so we shall continue to play our play alone for ourselves as before." To this the men answered:

"If any woman plays Ekkpo Njawhaw again she shall be bound to a stake in the market-place and be beheaded before all the townsfolk, that other women may see her fate and learn to play no more."

In spite of this the old women still continued to carry out the rites as before, hidden in the bush in a secret place which they had made. After long searching, however, the men found them and bore them off to Oduko market-place where their heads were struck off in the sight of the trembling women.

That is the reason why none but men may join the play of Ekkpo Njawhaw, or even witness the rites of this society.

After this change had been made therefore, all the inhabitants of a town who did not belong to the cult were ordered to keep within their houses, behind shut doors and windows, while the images ran up and down.

Not long ago at Ndiya, a woman, Adiaha Udaw Anwa by name, dared to sit on her veranda and watch the forbidden sight. The "image" ran in to catch and punish her for her temerity. Terrified at the consequences of her curiosity the poor woman ran inside the house and fastened the door, but the followers of Ekkpo soon forced open this frail barrier. Adiaha looked round for a hiding-place, and, in default of a better, climbed into the cupboard over the hearth where pots and pans are kept and meat is laid for smoking. The bottom of this receptacle is never solid but made of palm stems, laid crosswise, so that the smoke may pass through the interstices. After Ekkpo Njawhaw had forced an entrance he could not for the moment see where the woman was hidden but heard the palm stems creaking beneath her weight, so slashed upward with his machet and cut through the bottom of the cupboard, so that she fell down.

He then struck her twice across the head, making two wounds, one running from above the root of the nose to the back of the skull, and the other from ear to ear across the crown, thus marking her with a great cross.

Later a native doctor took the woman in hand, and cured her wounds after a long course of treatment, but the hair has never grown again over the scars, which are still clearly to be seen.

Another case concerned a little girl about eight years of age, also named Adiaha, who was rescued from being offered up to Ekkpo Njawhaw, after the sacrificial dress had been actually placed upon her. [35]

This Ibibio story of the revolt of man calls to mind a similar state of things, the memory of which is celebrated at the Fuegian festival, Kina. This was instituted to commemorate the rising of the males against the women "who formerly had the authority and possessed the secrets of sorcery." [36]

Just as behind the whole Ibibio pantheon looms the awful figure of "The Great Creatrix," so behind the cult of Ekkpo Njawhaw looms the still more terrible presence of Eka Ekkpo--Eka Abassi's dread counterpart--the source of all evil, the Death Bringer and Fount of Terror. The word Ekkpo does not only mean "ghosts," it also signifies "devils," and just as in Isaiah, chapter xlv., verse 7, we read "I form the light, and create darkness; I make peace and create evil: I the Lord do all these things," so here, amid these rude Ibibios, where woman is now regarded as a mere slave of her overlord man and one would least look for such a state of things, we get not fatherhood but motherhood --"motherhood, immaculate and alone a virgin birth"--as the source of the powers both of light and of darkness, of good and evil, of life and of death.

"Terrible indeed to look upon is this Mother of Ekkpo Njawhaw. Often of colossal size, ill proportioned and coal black in colour, she looms from out the darkness at the back of her sons' shrine, surrounded with the dreadful insignia of the cult, and with arms outstretched as if to welcome fresh victims. Around her flat, misshapen feet lie skulls, some new and ivory tinted, some blackened with the smoke of many sacrifices, and others carved with astonishing care and fidelity from solid blocks of wood. Two sons she has Akpan Njawhaw, the first-born, and Udaw, the second-born; also two daughters--Adiaha, the elder, and Angwa-Angwa, the younger.

"At the planting of farms the lesser rites of the cult are carried out; but the greater ceremonies take place at the New Yam Festival. Eight days before the first of the new season's crop may be eaten, in any town where this society has gained a footing, the images must be carried forth in solemn procession and set up in the public square." [37]

On such occasions the figure of Eka Ekkpo stands in the midst, with a son on either hand. Sometimes the effigies of the two daughters are placed there in addition, one at each end of the family line. For the first seven days, at dusk each evening, fowls and other offerings are brought and offered up before the fetishes, while the club drums are beaten to warn non-members among the passers-by from venturing too near the sacred spot. No yams may be brought on this occasion, and as is but meet, victims are first offered to Eka Ekkpo, seeing that she is the fount from which the others have sprung. Akpan is the next to receive offerings, then comes the turn of Udaw, and lastly the two daughters, though these are sometimes neglected altogether.

On the eighth day the images are carried back to their usual abode, that of "the Mother" being borne in front. Should anyone chance to meet this terrible procession upon the road, the first thing that a native would do would be to look whether the fetish was represented with one ear or two. In the latter case there would be a chance of life, because the goddess might possibly listen to the victim's frenzied prayer for mercy. In the former case prayer would be useless, because with one ear (Una Utung) she cannot listen to anyone. Only with two ears is it possible for her to have compassion.

To primitive races, and indeed the world over, death must always be one of the great mysteries, and it is the less astonishing that for Ibibios the supreme ruler of the Ghost Realm should be feminine when we consider that according to some peoples, for instance the Yaos and Wayisa of East Central Africa, death itself "was originally brought into the world by a woman who taught two men to go to sleep. One day, while they slumbered, she held the nostrils of one of them till his breath ceased, and he died." [38]

As has already been mentioned, if a woman chanced to witness an Ekkpo Njawhaw play, no matter how unwillingly, a member was singled out, and robed with all haste in the special dress of the cult executioner. After the poor woman he crept, "softly, softly," and exacted a terrible penalty for her unwitting trespass. No Ekkpo "image" may go forth without a machet in his hand. Each, therefore, is ready at a moment's notice to fulfil the behest of the "Great Mother," and, like the devotees of Kali Ma, bring to her shrine "Gobbets fresh and fresh!"

Chance also brought to light the fact that even over the "Great Warriors Club"--Ekong--(i.e. War) woman was once the dominating influence. This is shown in a curious survival.

At the time of the new yam harvest the members of "Ekong" assemble for an interesting ceremony. Across a corner of one of the town "playgrounds" a line of forked sticks is driven into the earth. This is so arranged that at the beginning and end of the row a great tree may usually be found. At the height of about four and a half feet from the ground, between the supports, palm leaves are hung, and against the terminal tree on the left-hand side is to be seen a little arbour made of the same leaves. In this a member of the society, chosen on account of his sweet voice, sits singing during the greater part of the ceremony. He is clothed in women's garments, and represents "The Mother of Ekong"; "For unless the latter be present on such an occasion, no blessing can be hoped for during the coming year."

So far as could be ascertained, Ekong also had no father, but sprang in full strength, it would appear, from beneath the heart of a virgin. It was very difficult to obtain any information on this subject, the tradition of which seems all but to have died out in the present day. Two very old women were, however, induced to relate what their grandmothers had told them as little children, and the account tallied in almost every particular, the only difference being that in one case my informant asserted that Ekong sprang forth "fully armed," Athene-like, from the body of his mother, and in the second case it was only said that he issued "in full strength, able to bear arms." The latter account was afterwards corroborated by Akpabio of Awa.

WOMAN IN WAR TIME

IN war time, even now, strong women on both sides act as scouts. They know that they will not be killed, so go before the main body fearlessly spying upon the enemy. As soon as the first sign of the latter is seen they cry out to warn their own men, and then run aside so as not to be in the way.

At times a band of Amazons comes across and captures a single foeman. Then these women, usually so gentle and kindly, seem to change their whole nature. They fall upon the luckless man, bind, and often cruelly wound him; then hand him over in triumph to be slain by the men of their own party.

Perhaps the most important service rendered by the women of the tribe in time of war is the carrying out of the secret rites decreed by ancient law for the burial of a warrior. As much as could be learnt of the matter from the men of the tribe is thus recorded:

"When a man in the prime of life is cut off in battle, the body is carried home to the dead man's town by wedded women who are his next of kin. No man may touch the corpse. Weeping and singing sad songs, it is borne by their gentle hands to a place of thick bush called owok afai--the forest of those slain by sudden death. . . . No maiden may be present at these rites; only to wives may such sad mysteries be revealed." [39]

Later, an ancient woman was induced to confide to me part at least of these strange rites. I had not intended to publish them, nor, indeed, much of the information already incorporated in the foregoing account. Certain English scientists, however, of the highest distinction, have been good enough to point out that the matter is not without ethnological interest, and also that it is most improbable that this little study will ever reach those in any way concerned. Save for one detail, therefore, all that could be gleaned on the subject is given here.

After the bodies of dead warriors have been borne into the shadows of that part of the forest set aside for this purpose, they are gently laid upon beds of fresh leaves, high piled to form a last couch, not far from the place where an open grave has been prepared. Young boughs are next picked from sacred trees, the names of which, unfortunately, my informant could not be persuaded to reveal. These boughs are drawn over the bodies of the slain amid low, wailing chants and fast-falling tears. The chants are said to contain a prayer that the virility of the warrior thus cut off in the pride of life and strength may not be lost, but rather should go forth to bless with increase the hearths, farms and byres of his own townsfolk.

My informant explained that she was only able to give vaguely the meaning of the chants sung on such occasions, since these have been handed down in a tongue so old as to be practically forgotten in the present day. It is a matter of great regret to us that the expense of transport in countries such as this, where all impedimenta must be borne upon carriers' heads, had hitherto kept us from adding a phonograph to the already somewhat long list of scientific apparatus which we are in the habit of carrying about with us. Lady Frazer, who has herself rendered such inestimable services to science, had urged us to do so, and had we but been able to follow her advice it might have been possible to secure records of these old songs, the chance to obtain which may in all probability never occur again. Alas! "Our Lady Poverty" is a hard task-mistress, and often places a stern veto upon the garnering of much of the rich harvest which, in Africa, lies on every hand awaiting gleaning.

Though the exact meaning of the ritual chants has now been lost, the idea underlying the ceremonies is indicated by the actions accompanying the song, as, for instance, when the sacred boughs are drawn over that part of the body regarded as the seat of virile energy, with the avowed purpose of withdrawing the spirit of fertility into the leaves. Before interment, small portions of the body are also cut away and placed, together with the sacred leaves, in earthen pots never before used. These are wrapped up in the garments of the celebrants, and borne forth by them in silence, to be secretly interred in farm or byre, or hidden away in holes dug beneath the hearth or bridal bed.

The reason that knowledge of such rites must be kept alike from men and maidens of the tribe is said to be that this secret was among those entrusted to women in the days when woman, not man, was the dominant sex, and that these were not disclosed at the time when males were initiated into the mysteries of the secret societies, because it had been revealed that on the guarding of this secret depended the strength of the tribe. Were the rites once disclosed the power of the juju would be broken, few or no babes would be born, farms and herds would yield but scanty increase, while the arms of future generations of fighting men would lose their strength and hearts their courage--until the Ibibio people were either enslaved or had vanished from the face of the earth.

During our last leave in England we had the privilege of talking over those primitive customs and beliefs which seemed to us of special interest with so great an authority as Dr. Wallis Budge, of the British Museum. Among other incidents he listened to that above given, and when the little account was finished pointed out the striking similarity between this still surviving rite and the strange story of the origin of Horus--that seed of life and love snatched by the widowed Isis from death itself. Indeed, were the account of this Ibibio rite given in full detail it might almost seem as though intended as a re-enactment of the ancient tragedy of the Nile, when the mighty goddess Isis found the body of the slaughtered Osiris, and by her knowledge of the mysteries of birth and death "the Great Mother" wrung a new life from out the very jaws of desolation and despair. [40]

At present there seems little danger of a falling off in numbers among Ibibios, for the greatest pride of both men and women is to become the parents of many children. The head chief of Oyubia, Enyenihi by name, has a family of thirty, all of whom he proudly claims as his own offspring. Large as the number seems, however, it is quite outdone by the crowd of children which surrounds many chiefs. Akpan Udaw Ibomm of Ikotobo, for instance, who died in 1913, had a hundred and sixty sons and daughters, of all of whom he claimed to be the actual father. Ofeok Oyo of Ikua Ita too, who has only lately died, was the mother of twenty fine children. Yet, almost to the day of her death she carried herself as straight and well and was as tall and good to look upon, according to native ideas, as many a woman who had borne but a single babe. Indeed the Ibibios and neighbouring peoples would seem to be a standing contradiction to the theory that polygamy tends to restrict the race. We were informed on the authority of Mr. John Bailey, a well-known native Government official, who was present when Sir Claude Macdonald went up to Afikpo, on the Cross River, that one chief alone brought ninety sons to salute the Chief Commissioner! True it is that the distinguished administrator himself, whose memory is held in grateful remembrance by European and native alike throughout the length and breadth of the colony for whose prosperity he did so much, thinks that nineteen would be a more probable number to give; but owing to the marriage customs and rules as to family membership it is by no means impossible that one chief should be able to produce the number stated.

Among some of the more civilised Efiks of Calabar the growth of the family seems to have been restricted, to a certain extent, from motives of vanity on the part of the women, who fear that much child-bearing might spoil their beauty. Yet, even here, there does not seem to be cause for anxiety as to the danger of racial suicide. The late Chief Esonta of Old Town, for instance, had forty-five wives, who, between them, are said to have borne him a hundred and sixty children!

Chief Essien Etim, who died in 1910, and was a well-known Calabar chief, is stated to have had ninety-nine sons and daughters. After his death, a dispute arose as to the distribution of the property, and the family marched into Court to lay the matter before His Honour Judge Weber. It was fortunate that the disagreement was only among themselves, so that litigation did not extend to another family of like or superior size.

Another well-known chief, Efa Etung Effion by name, had sixty wives and ninety-five piccans; while Chief Abassi Okun Abassi of Creek Town had a mere thirty-five to show; but then he had only seven wives all told! The aforementioned numbers are given on the authority of Chief Daniel Henshaw.

To a certain extent large families may be accounted for by the custom which, on the death of a chief, caused the wives to be divided out among sons and brothers, who henceforth assumed towards them the position formerly held by the deceased; care being taken that a woman should not thus be given to her own son. Before death a man usually "makes his will," under which term is included the disposal of his wives and female dependents. The women of the household are called before him on his death-bed, and he there and then decides to which relative each should be given. Often in this way a grown woman is allocated as "wife" to a small boy of eight or nine years old. In such a case all children which she may bear to other men, while the child-husband is growing up, are looked upon as his. So that, supposing some half-dozen women are bequeathed in this manner to a boy of eight, the latter on reaching the age of twelve might easily find himself titular "father" of a dozen or more children.

A case illustrating such a "marriage" came before the Native Court at Idua Oron. In this the plaintiff, Akon Abassi, stated on oath:

"My former husband died and left behind him a young brother of about ten years of age. According to his will I was betrothed to the latter, but as I was over twenty years old and already a mother I asked the parents of the child-husband to receive back their dowry, because the boy was too young for me."

A similar case occurred at the same sitting in which a woman named Kadu claimed divorce from a small boy, Affion Usuk Inyi by name. In the course of her evidence the plaintiff stated:

"About six and a half years ago I came out of the Fatting-house and was married. Not long afterwards my husband died, and I was told to become the wife of a boy about twelve years of age. I am now almost twenty-five years old, and therefore summon the defendant to receive back his dowry and set me free, as the child is too young to be my husband."

Many cases are known, however, in which young and attractive women have refused the advances of other wooers, and preferred to wait until the youth, to whom they have been given by the Will of their late husband, should be of sufficient age to wed them.

WIDOWHOOD AND BURIAL CUSTOMS

AMONG the Ibibios different funeral rites are prescribed according to age, position, and manner of death.

To begin with the youngest. The bodies of babes who die within a few days of birth may not be buried like those to whom a fuller span of life was given, but are laid in an earthen bowl which is then placed, inverted, in a shallow hole scooped out by the side of the road.

A somewhat similar custom is reported from among the Baganda for the burial of a twin. "The embalmed body was wrapped round with a creeper and put into a new cooking-pot. When the preparations were complete, the relations assembled, a man called the 'Mutaka' took the corpse to waste land near a main road, dug the grave, and laid the body in it; on the grave he placed a cooking-pot mouth downwards, but put no earth in. Then everyone who passed by knew the place to be the grave of a twin, and avoided it lest the ghost should catch them. Women especially avoided the place and threw grass upon the grave to prevent the ghost from entering into them and being reborn." [41]

Any such upturned pots may be seen along the paths near Akaiya, especially those leading through parts of the bush which are carefully shunned at nightfall, for there the bodies of all who have died of smallpox, leprosy, or other infectious disease are flung and left without burial. An almost similar fate befalls those of women who have died in or immediately before childbirth, since these, too, are regarded as unclean. Should such a one die before giving birth, her body is cut open and the fœtus carefully removed and interred in an inverted pot in the manner described. As with those who died in childbirth, the corpse is propped against a tree and left, with sunk head and hanging hands, until the luxuriant vegetation mercifully covers the pitiful remains with its green mantle.

The ghosts of such are greatly feared, as much here and now as amid the ancient Babylonians, among whose most dreaded wraiths are mentioned:

> "A woman that hath died in travail,
> Or a woman that hath died with a babe at the breast,
> Or a weeping woman that hath died with a babe at the breast." [42]

When the bearers come back after disposing of these pitiful dead they may not enter their houses, but must wait outside that of the dead woman, until the members of her family have brought out and sacrificed a dog, a cock, and some eggs. Magic leaves are ground between stones and rubbed upon the bodies of the corpse bearers, while the kinsmen pray that this so sad a fate may never again overtake one of their house. The fowl's head is struck off, and its blood sprinkled over the bearers, who chant meanwhile:

> "Let not the evil thing pass from me to any woman."

Until the sacrifices have been made and the prayers offered, none who took part in carrying the corpse may touch a woman lest that which cut off the newly dead should be communicated to the living.

The attitude of mind which thus denies gentle burial to those who have known the pangs, without the joys, of motherhood, is far as the poles asunder from that expressed by the old northern ballad in which so different a fate is meted out:

> Their beds are made in Heaven high,
> Full lowly down by our dear Lord's knee,
> All girt about wi' gilly flowers,
> A right fair company for to see." [43]

Yet, though among Ibibios but little sentiment is wasted on these unfortunates, their lot, in the old days at least, was happier than that of women unlucky enough to bear twins. The fate of such has already been described, and the ill-results of the cruel superstition do not cease with life, but are thought to continue even after death. A woman who dies in giving birth to twins, or before the end of her year of purification after such an event, may not be carried to her last resting-place through the house door, any more than she may go out by it on leaving home to spend the prescribed twelve moons in the twin women's town. Such sad exiles must pass through a hole purposely broken in the wall, by which exit the unfortunate babes are also carried forth. Further, the body of a twin mother may on no account be borne along a road by which ordinary people pass to and fro, but only by a little path specially cut through the bush to the place where it is to be flung.

The reason for this prohibition is much the same as that given in Cambodia for carrying a dead body feet foremost, i.e. "that it may not see the house, in which event other sickness and other deaths would result." Ibibios say, too, that should the ghost return and try to enter her former home she would be unable to do so since the place by which the body was carried forth has been blocked up, and wraiths can only enter by the same way through which their bodies were borne forth-the converse of that law of the spirit world explained by Mephistopheles to Faust--

> "For goblins and for spectres it is law
> That where we enter in, there also we withdraw." [44]

In the country round Awa, a superstition obtains much like that of the Malayan "langsuir," a description of which is thus given by Sir William Maxwell:

"If a woman dies in childbirth either before delivery or after the birth of a child, and before the forty days of uncleanness have expired, she is popularly supposed to become a 'langsuyar,' a flying demon of the nature of the 'White Lady' or 'Banshee.' To prevent this a quantity of glass beads are put in the mouth of the corpse, a hen's egg is put under each armpit, and needles are placed in the palms of the hands. It is believed that if this is done the dead woman cannot become a langsuyar, as she cannot open her mouth to shriek (ngilai) or wave her arms as wings, or open and shut her hands to assist her flight."

It was only with great difficulty that any information could be gleaned as to this terrible wraith, since it is a matter of firm belief that even to mention her might lay the speaker open to an unwelcome visitation. No entreaty or inducement which we could offer availed to persuade any informant to confide to us the appellation by which these ghastly and malignant spirits are known. The utmost we could prevail upon anyone to impart on the subject was that among some tribes she was called Ekwensu; we have since learned that this is the Ibo term for these sad wraiths. It was stated from several sources that, by simply calling aloud the dread name, a discarded wife had succeeded in drawing down upon her husband the curse of such an uncanny housemate. After long seeking we learnt, however, that in this part of the world when a woman has died in childbirth, the mouth of the corpse is closed with pitch, and this mixed with thorns is sometimes also placed beneath the armpits, while the hands are occasionally bound to the sides. To be efficacious this service should be rendered by an old woman, "who must be such a one as had brought many children into the world but has now long ceased from bearing." No mention was made of other precautions, such as beads, eggs, or needles placed in the palms.

These sad wraiths are thought to be filled with enmity against the whole human race, because they have been robbed of offspring and denied burial, in consequence of which last misfortune they are forced to wander up and down over the length and breadth of the earth, racked with hunger and parched with thirst, with no resting-place in the ghost town amid kindly kith and kin. With the idea of avenging themselves upon men for this dreary lot they sometimes take the form of a beautiful woman in order to attract the regard of a lover. To such the wraith may bear elfin children, and is even said to be capable of so well disguising her evil nature as to live among mortals unsuspected for years. Only one peculiarity does she show. She cannot join in the merrymakings of her town, for, should she once be inveigled into a circle of dancers, her feet skim the earth so lightly that she can no longer keep to the ground, but is forced to spring--ever higher and higher--till at last, with a blood-curdling shriek, she flies away, and is even said at times, to the horror of the spectators, to have changed before their eyes into the form of an owl or vampire bat.

When a man has fallen under the spell of one of these terrible beings he is lost indeed, for at death the ghoul-wife and her demon offspring gather round his bed, mopping and mowing, and their unclean presence keeps off the kindly spirits of those ancestors whom he would fain join in the ghost town.

Further details of the "langsuir," corresponding in many points with those given above, may be found in the fascinating pages of Skeat's "Malay Magic." The passage is quoted in full on account of its charm

The original langsuir, whose embodiment is supposed to be a kind of night owl, is described as being a woman of dazzling beauty who died from the shock of hearing that her child was stillborn and had taken the shape of the pontianak or mati-anak--a kind of night owl. On hearing this terrible news she clapped her hands, and without further warning flew whinnying away to a tree, upon which she perched. She may be known by her robe of green, by her tapering nails of extraordinary length (a mark of beauty), and by the long jet black tresses which she allows to fall down to her ankles--only alas! (for the truth must be told) in order to conceal the hole in the back of her neck through which she sucks the blood of children! These vampire-like proclivities of hers may, however, be successfully combated if the right means are adopted, for if you are able to catch her, cut short her nails and luxuriant tresses, and stuff them into the hole in her neck, she will become tame and indistinguishable from an ordinary woman, remaining so for years. Cases have been known, indeed, in which she has become a wife and a mother, until she was allowed to dance at a village merrymaking, when she at once reverted to her ghostly form and flew off into the dark and gloomy forest from whence she came."

Of the pontianak or mati-anak, i.e. the ghost of a stillborn child, no trace could be found among the Ibibios, and no special precaution save that of burying face downwards beneath an inverted bowl, seemed taken to prevent its return.

The following story was told by an Efik woman to whom it was related by a friend who lived near the Opobo border:

"Many, many years ago a very beautiful woman lived upon earth. She married a great chief who loved her beyond all his other wives. To her alone he gave the gifts which should have been shared between all of them, and neglected the rest for her sake. This made the others so jealous that they consulted together and bought a strong juju which they buried one night beneath the path by which the favoured wife went to her farm. Further, they tied pieces of tie-tie into strong knots and hid them beneath her bed, and locked and clasped door- and box-locks, that by this magic the portals of birth should be closed against the coming of any babe to her.

"By this means the woman was kept childless for many years, but at length her husband collected great gifts and took them to a very strong juju, thereby purchasing a medicine which he brought back and gave, in all secrecy, to this best-loved wife. By its strength the bad jujus were overcome, and the fellow-wives saw that their envious plots were vain.

"Now among the number was a witch. Full of malice therefore, she went before her witch company and told how her rival had triumphed over the magic knots and other spells wrought against her, and was about to bear a babe. Then all the witches plotted together to weave a most evil charm, by means of which the babe should meet death on life's threshold. Thus it came to pass, and when the little dead form was shown to the mother she gave but one cry, and striking out with her hands as though to fend off the cruel fellow-wives, without further warning flew up into the branches of a tall tree, upon which she perched in the guise of a white owl, uttering plaintive cries. So embittered was she by the treatment she had received that whenever one of her enemies bore a babe she used to come down at night time and, vampire-like, suck its essence, so that it also died."

It is interesting to compare this Ibibio version with those from the Malay States given previously.

Little children from one to seven years of age are laid in the grave on their right side, as if sleeping, with hands folded palm to palm and placed between the knees. Should it happen that several piccans have died in any family one after the other on reaching about eight to ten years, the next child to expire at this age is also buried face downwards, "so that he may not see the way to be born again." It is thought that his spirit is one of those mischievous sprites who only reincarnate to bring grief to parents, and would never grow up to be a comfort to them in later years. The mother or grandmother of such unwelcome revenants usually breaks a finger or slits an ear of the corpse before it is laid in the grave, that, when it is born again, they may know it at once because it will bear this mark. The spirits are said to dislike this treatment so much "that they often give up their bad habit of dying, and on the next reincarnation grow up like other people."

When such a boy or girl has died the parents usually wash the feet and hands of the corpse and pour the water into a bottle which is kept in a corner of their sleeping-room. When the wife feels that she is once more about to become a mother, the liquid is sprinkled over the floor of the room, while the parents cry aloud the name of the ghost, saying, "You must not be born into our family again."

Among the Ekets the father of a child is held responsible for its burial. It is a breach of custom for the mother to lay it in the grave. A case illustrating this came before the Native Court at Eket early in April, 1913, in which the plaintiff stated:

"Defendant married my daughter. They had a child who died. Just before its death defendant came in and found the dying child in my arms. At once he caught up a machet, and with the flat of this struck me across the mouth. I said to him 'What have I done?' He did not answer, but took up a jar of palm wine which stood near by and flung the contents over the `Mbiam juju crying, 'Let me die for my child!' I said to the people who stood around, 'He thinks that I am killing the child, but never have I heard of a grandmother who harmed her grandchild!' Then I got up and went away, leaving the babe with its mother. I did not go far, but came back into the courtyard and made a fire in a corner, out of the way, thinking 'I will stay here till I know how it goes with the child.' As I sat waiting and listening, defendant came out, seized me by foot and throat, and flung me out of the compound. He caught up his machet and would have killed me, but the bystanders ran between and stopped him from harming me further. It was then that the child died, and so soon as he knew that its soul had quite gone from it he thrust the dead body into the arms of my daughter, and bade her bear it to my house. This she did, and he refused to bury it, although it is our custom for the father to bury dead babes. It is unseemly and against our rule that a woman should do so, yet when the husband's half-brother came and ordered my daughter to bring the dead body and bury it, she obeyed. She it was, therefore, the mother, who laid it in the grave."

In the course of my husband's study of native burial rites he stumbled upon the discovery that among the Ibos underground chambers, much on the plan of those of ancient Egypt, were formerly prepared for the reception of the dead. In talking over the matter with an Efik chief of high standing the latter stated that in olden days at Calabar graves only slightly different in form used to be dug out for the interment of chiefs. His description was as follows:

"Within the walls of the dead man's compound an oblong chamber often twenty-four feet deep, was dug. Through one of the sides they cut a tunnel, and at the end of this a large underground room was hollowed out. . . . . When all had been arranged the coffin was carefully lowered into the first chamber, borne through the passage, and laid upon the resting-place so reverently prepared.

"Then the best-loved wife of the deceased and two of his most beautiful slaves were led into the chamber and seated upon three chairs at the feet of, and facing, their dead lord. Between living and dead a table was placed, and on this dish es containing fine 'chop' was set.

"The best-loved wife was in the centre, and into her hands a lighted lamp was given. Then all save the three women left the burial room. Boards were placed before the entrance and earth piled against these until the passage was filled up. Bolts of cloth and the less costly articles, were then laid in the first compartment, immediately beneath the shaft. Lastly soil was thrown in and beaten down over all." [45]

WIDOWHOOD AND BURIAL CUSTOMS (CONTINUED)

FROM the moment when the death of a great Efik chief was announced his widows came under the care of the Ndito Than society, known among Ibibios by the name of "Iban Isong," i.e. Women of the Soil. Should an unfortunate widow offend against custom in any way, such as by washing face or feet, or plaiting her hair, the society at once fined her; for members were continually passing in and out of the house of mourning to watch that the rules were observed. At cock-crow each day the women of the household had to wake and start crying for an hour or two, and should one of them not be thought to perform her part of the ceremony in a sufficiently energetic manner, external aids were applied of sufficient strength to remedy any lack of naturalness. Widows were not allowed to leave the compound on any pretext, but were forced to stay, each in her own house, sitting upon a small mat in a dark corner. No covering was permitted, save the narrow strip usually worn round the waist beneath the robe and called the "woman's cloth."

When women from other families came, the visitors seated themselves just before their hostess. No sooner had they settled down than the widow started to weep anew, and the guests joined her in lamentation. After a certain time spent in this way they went on to another wife, and so on till all had been condoled with. Sisters and cousins of the dead man usually received visits in the room beneath the floor of which the corpse was buried.

Only legal wives were thus secluded. Other women of the household, no matter how near or dear they might have been to the dead, were not expected to stay in their little corners, but were free to come and go within the compound. The time of seclusion was called that of the "Mbuk Pisi" house, i.e. house of mourning.

When a very great chief dies his widows make a certain offering to the Ndito Than Society. For this purpose they prepare long wrappings of silk, and, after having presented these, send to inform their families of the bereavement which has befallen them. In olden days a year or more was usually spent in this seclusion. Now it is only a week or two, or at most a month.

As the time of mourning drew to an end, about nine o'clock one night a cry was heard coming from the Egbo house. This was the signal for the beginning of what was called a very "strong night" at Calabar. All the widows stepped, one by one, out of the compound where they had so long been confined, and proceeded to the Egbo shed, each with her family walking round her like a fence The building was full of the great chiefs of the town, while crowds of spectators stood outside. After all the wives had been stationed before the entrance, the name of each was called in turn, from the lowest to the highest, with the words:

"You must 'cry' your husband before the Egbo, that Egbo may hear."

Then, in the stillness, the poor woman raised her voice bewailing her loss, and the Egbo answered the cry from within, "a very thick and heavy sound amid the silence." After awhile came a pause, then all began again as before. Seven times the wail rose; but the seventh was the last. All this time the family of the first woman stood in readiness to pass her along from one to another. Suddenly bells were heard ringing, and the widow started to run, sheltered always by her kinsfolk. The same happened to all in turn, and, should some unfortunate woman have no strong family to encircle and save her, Egbo caught her and she died there and then.

After having "cried their husband before the Egbo," the widows went back once more to the house of mourning, and early next day Idemm Ikwaw (i.e. lesser Egbo) came out and went round the town. All the principal chiefs followed him, holding in their hands twenty to forty young palm stems, each about four feet long, from which the hard skin had been stripped off, so that only the soft inner part was left.

When these had gathered in the courtyard, the women came out from the Mbuk Pisi house one by one with folded arms and stepping backwards "softly, softly"; for they might not turn their heads. Each was shaking with terror, for none knew what was coming and they feared "too much." All around them bells were ringing with deafening clang and bang. The Egbo image struck at each, as she came forth, and, if the woman was lithe and nimble of mind as well as body, at the first stroke she sprang back into the house, but many were too bewildered to know where to turn. For each blow a new stick was used, the others being thrown away immediately. After every widow had been struck in turn, the ceremony was over. "The minds of the women could rest in peace now. There was nothing more to fear."

Later in the day all went down to the river to bathe. There they washed the little cloths which had so long been worn unchanged, and shaved their heads. "Each widow was laved by the women of her family and those who were her dearest friends. No man could see them walking unrobed because of the press of women about each. After bathing they dressed themselves in cloth woven of plaited grasses, the fine kind called Ofon Ndam, black, red, and yellow in colour, which is as soft as linen." Then the "woman's cloth," and every spoon, calabash and other utensil used during the time of mourning was thrown into the river; were this not done it was thought that their continued possession would entail barrenness upon their owner. After these had been cast away the widows returned for the last time to the house of their late husband. They did not enter, however, but only sat on the veranda.

Next some of the principal women of the town and five or six chiefs went thither as witnesses that all had "cleansed themselves," and now wished to go back to the homes of their fathers. The household juju was brought out and set upon the ground, and before it each widow took oath:

"During my husband's lifetime if I was unfaithful to him or did any bad thing against his family may the juju punish me! If not, may I go clear!"

After this each woman's kin surrounded her. She raised her clasped hands above her head, resting them with interlocked fingers upon the crown, and cried, "My husband divorces me to-day!" The spectators took up the cry, calling in chorus upon the dead man by his "fine names" such as "Helper of the Town," etc.

After each widow had thus set herself free, the household dependents came forward and "cried" in much the same manner. Then the "free born" amongst them all went back to the homes of their fathers.

For seven days only the native grass cloth "Ofon Ndam" might be worn by the bereaved women, and, when this was laid aside, custom ordained that a kind called "Isodoho" should be substituted.

Sisters, cousins, and women "members" of the deceased's family wore a blue cloth two fathoms long, knotted over the left shoulder and hanging straight down like the usual farm dress. As a further sign of mourning they used to grind charcoal and mix with a little oil to form a black pigment, with which they painted a mark from temple to temple across the forehead, much in the shape of a crescent moon. It is quite probably from this circumstance that the "house of mourning" among the Ibibios is termed "the moon house," though, when the supposition was mentioned, some of my informants disclaimed all knowledge of the point.

Male members of the family or household were supposed to wear black or dark blue cloth, sometimes for as much as a year and a half, until a date was fixed upon by the principal men among them, who said, "On such and such a day we will finish mourning." They liked to arrange so that this "throwing off of mourning" took place about Christmas time, before the planting of new farms.

It would seem that the period of mourning is purposely made as disagreeable as possible for the widows, in order to deter these from the temptation to poison their husbands so as to clear the way for another suitor.

As with the Greeks of old, both men and women shaved their heads in sign of mourning. Like the widows, some of the dependents wore Isodoho cloth, and some a kind dyed a lighter shade of blue called "Utan Okpo."

From the day when the widows "took oath before the juju" and returned to their fathers' homes they were free to marry again. [46]

On the occasion of the funeral rites of the head chief of Ikotobo, the cattle offered to the "Manes" of the dead were laid out to the left of the throne upon which the corpse sat in state; while on the right, as if to balance the slaughtered sheep, which in this case were twenty in number, crouched the deceased's twenty wives with their children, all wailing and wringing their hands. But for the presence of the "white man," [47] most, if not all, of these unfortunate women would have been sacrificed also and buried with their lord. Even as it was their fate was sad enough. They were painted over with black pigment and forced to go into mourning for six months, though in the case of lesser men the period is sometimes shortened to as little as seven days. During this time they were obliged to observe the strictest seclusion. On such occasions none is allowed to wash either body or clothes. They are even forbidden to stand at the door of their prison while rain is falling, lest a single drop should touch them and thus cleanse a fractional part of the body. During this time the wretched women exist under conditions too hideous for description. At the end of their seclusion the Egbo "images" come with attendants and drive them forth from the dead man's house, which is then broken down. Images and attendants bear sharp machets, with which they slash the arms of the terrified women, who run weeping to seek out former friends and beg them to bind up their wounds. After this they remain homeless until parcelled out among the heirs of the dead man.

The wives of even poor Ibibios must remain secluded for a week after their husband's burial. During this time they may wear no garment save a small loin cloth and a piece of goat's skin tied over the right hand. [48] Before coming forth they are allowed to dress their hair, bathe and resume their customary garments. The first use they make of freedom is usually to go and pluck themselves boughs of ntung leaves, which they wave to and fro "to drive away the scent of the ghost," for Ibibios, like the ancient Babylonians, believe that ghosts have a very evil smell. Thus protected, the women approach the grave and lay upon it, folded into a small roll, the cloth and piece of skin which they have worn during the time of their seclusion. After this has been duly done they may return to their ordinary mode of life, mixing with their fellows and going to market as before.

In the neighbourhood of Awa when a chief fell sick his nearest kinsmen used to go to the Idiong priest and ask the cause of the illness. Should the oracle declare, as was usually the case, that this had been brought about in consequence of a wife's unfaithfulness, Idiong was next asked to point out the guilty woman. So soon as her name was pronounced she was called upon to confess and give the name of her lover. Should she refuse and as a result, according to general opinion, the husband died, the oracle was consulted once more, and, on the almost invariable pronouncement that the woman was guilty of the death, a meeting of the townsfolk was called to decide upon her fate. By ancient custom this might be meted out in two ways; either she was buried alive by the dead man's side, in place of a female slave usually sacrificed on such an occasion, or forced to sit above the grave. In the latter case a slender pole of hard wood was brought, sharpened to a fine point before the eyes of the wretched woman, and then driven into the skull, right through the body, and deep down into the earth, in such a manner as to impale her above the place of burial.

Before killing such victims the people used to gather round and order them to pronounce a blessing upon the town. "Make plenty piccans be born to us," they would cry; "plenty girls and plenty boys." Should the victim refuse to repeat the words they coaxed her, and said:

"If you will but speak this blessing we will let you go free."

Should she again refuse they beat her very cruelly, crying, "Now speak." If, despite the pain, she still refused, the "fearful Egbo" would come out--hideous beyond description--and threaten nameless tortures till she yielded.

In some rare cases the woman has still been known to hold out, as is also recorded of one or other of the slaves ordained by custom to share the grave of their lord, and from whom a like "blessing" was demanded. Under such circumstances the victims were never sacrificed, since to do so would have been to draw down a period of barrenness and poverty upon the town. Instead of killing such steadfast souls, therefore, they were sold into slavery, while a victim who could be forced or cajoled into pronouncing the necessary formula was offered instead.

It was of the utmost importance to the well-being of the spirits of parents in the Ghost Realm that a son should be left behind who would carry out the burial rites with all due observances. The straits to which good sons were sometimes put in order to make sure that the necessary ritual was performed are illustrated by the story of the sham burial of the mother of the head chief of Ikot Okudum--a town not far from Ubium Creek.

Many years ago when the present head chief, Etuk Udaw Akpan by name, was a young man, he was very strong and brave. For a certain reason his fellow-townsmen wanted to kill him. They tried their best, and set many snares, but lie always escaped them.

One day he went to visit the house of a friend in the Ubium country. His host prepared "chop" and set it before him, with palm wine and all things necessary for the refreshment of an honoured guest. During the meal his enemies heard that he was within, so they sent a message to the owner of the compound, saying:

"For a long time we have wanted to kill this man but could never catch him. We beg you, therefore, to give him into our hands, and in return we will pay you a great sum."

The host said, "I agree, provided the amount you offer is large enough!" So they brought much money, whereon he said, "It is good. Do to him what you will."

Then the people surrounded the house and fastened the doors of the encircling fence so that Etuk might not escape them. When all was ready they called:

"Come out. We wish to ask you a word." He, however, answered, "No. If you have anything to say, it can be said while I am within." The people replied, "You must come out." Then when they found that he would not do this, they tried to force in the door and fall upon him.

On that Etuk drew out a sharp machet which was hidden beneath his gown, and springing through the door shut it suddenly behind him, and stood facing his foes. So unexpected was his appearance, and so fierce his blows, that momentarily the people all gave way before him. At a glance he saw that the gates were barred, so, as he was an excellent climber, before anyone could stop him, he sprang upon the mud wall of the veranda and thence to the roof. Along this he rushed till he came to a place where the building was very near the fence, cleared this at a bound, and alighted safely on the other side.

Then he ran for his life toward the bush, crying out, "If you want me, follow me now!"

It was some time before those within the enclosure could unbar the gate which they themselves had so carefully fastened, and by the time this was done Etuk had disappeared.

All day he hid, but after nightfall managed to reach his home unnoticed. There he said to his mother:

"To-day I went to a house in the Ubium country, whither the townsmen followed to kill me. I was very sorry for myself and also for you, because you are my mother and, unless I am killed, you will probably die before me. In that case it would be my duty to bury you. Now that they want to kill me so soon I fear that you may be left with no grown-up son to perform the rites for you, since my brothers are still very young. I think, there-fore, it is best, while there is yet time, to call all the townsfolk together and do that which is proper for a son to do for a dead mother."

To this the woman answered, "Do as you say, for the people want to kill you, and leave me alone in the world with no one to bury me when my time shall come."

Then Etuk sent one of his small brothers to summon the townsfolk. Goats, cows and much mimbo had been provided, together with everything necessary to do honour to a dead woman.

When all were assembled before the house Etuk said to his mother, "Go now and bathe." Then when the bath was finished he robed her as is done with a corpse. Afterwards he went outside and placed a chair for his mother, who sat thereon in the sight of all the people, as the dead are used to sit in state.

Next all the beasts were slaughtered, and Etuk Udaw took the blood and poured it out before the feet of his mother, as is customary for women who leave behind them a son of fitting age to carry out the burial rites. When this was finished he ordered the people to play the death play for his mother, and at the end bade her go back into the house while he addressed the company.

First he told them to keep silence for a while, and then asked:

"Do you know what I mean by dressing my mother like a dead woman and holding her burial rites while she is still alive?" They answered, "No, we cannot even guess, though we question much among our selves on this very matter." So he continued:

"You want to kill me, and should I die before her she would be left in the world without a son old enough to bury her properly when the time comes. Therefore I have done all this before you slay me, that everything may be performed in due order and she may not suffer in the Ghost Realm."

They answered, "We have drunk all this mimbo and eaten these sacrifices to no purpose as it appears! Never have we seen such a thing as this!" So they went away, much amazed. Nevertheless, from that time they left the man in peace, and did not strive to harm him as they had before.

Not long afterwards one of the small brothers fell ill, so Etuk went to the Idiong man and asked the reason. The diviner consulted the oracle, and replied:

"It is because you have carried out the death rites of your mother, and the evil spirits grow impatient, watching for her to die. As she has not yet reached the ghost town, they are trying to take one of your young brothers."

On hearing this, Etuk went home and bought many medicines, he also offered sacrifices to save the boy, but in spite of all that was done the little one died.

The mother herself lived for many, many years. Indeed, it is only about four years since she went to the ghost town, but the son still lives, and has become head chief over all those who formerly wished to kill him, and he now sits as a "member," judging cases in the Eket Native Court.

L'ENVOI

Degema, Nigeria.
June, 1911

SUCH, from cradle to grave, is the life story of an Ibibio woman, so far as those of her people were willing to confide it to one of an alien race. It is naturally a matter of regret that, owing to the fear of being blamed by their kin for having imparted so much information to a stranger, hardly one of my informants would allow her name to be given as authority for any statement here set down. When, however, men and women can be brought to grasp the fact, to which some natives with more than a veneer of education are gradually awakening, that Africans have a great deal more to win than lose by placing on record old customs and beliefs before these are over-whelmed by the oncoming waves of alien religion and culture, the greatest stumbling-block will have been removed from the path of inquirers. It is true that there is much of barbarity and hideous cruelty in these ancient ceremonies, which the civilised negro would fain hide from the knowledge of white races, but it is doubtful whether there is anything more terrible to be disclosed concerning the fetish rites of West Africa than those known to have been practised in the early stages of all the great religions of the world, as witness Egyptian and Babylonian bas-reliefs. Yet, side by side with much that will be found revolting to twentieth century ideas, there yet remain traces of traditions and beliefs of a depth and value to which northern races are only just awakening.

Again, at the present day, whether we sympathise with or decry the feminist movement, the fact remains that, for good or ill, a spirit of restlessness has swept over the women of the world. A stirring and quickening has come to them, rousing a consciousness of power long latent which, rightly directed, may suffice to destroy pitfalls and sweep clean those foul places which now surround the path of the poor and weak, but which, wrongly guided, might lead along unlovely roads to sex antagonism and barren hate. The condition of many an African tribe of to-day is in all essentials the same as that through which we ourselves once passed in long-forgotten ages. Surely then, on whichever side we stand in the vexed question of the hour, [49] it is well for us to look back now and again and watch how primitive woman held her own, or learn what yet remains to be gleaned of the stages by which she rose to dominion over, or sank to serfdom beneath, the men of her day.

While re-reading these pages before sending them to press, news came that two women, splendidly trained and equipped, have set out to do, in another quarter of the globe, what is so inadequately attempted here. Perhaps, later on, others as well fitted as they may be induced to turn their attention to the women of Africa.

To my critics I would say that the first steps along a road, which to a certain extent at least has hitherto remained untrodden, are necessarily difficult and uncertain, and that only the intense interest which such a study has for us and the more than kindness of those whose opinion we so greatly value has emboldened me, in default of one more fitted, to attempt even so inadequate an account of these primitive women.

Perhaps a few words on another subject may be permitted here. A recent visitor to the coast wrote on her return reproaching her countrymen because so few English officials take their wives to West Africa, while many French and Germans do so. In discussing the matter with a German acquaintance on one of the boats, she quotes him as saying, apropos of the presence of white women, "It is only the English who fear the rains"--and herself adds in comment, "I deplored, though I could not resent, the slight touch of contempt in his tone."

Had this gifted authoress been aware of the true state of the case, and known how many men fruitlessly apply year after year for permission to bring their wives, she could have removed a misapprehension from the mind of her fellow-traveller, and would herself have had nothing to deplore on this score with regard to her countrymen save their misfortune in being deprived of those whose companionship they eagerly desire. Of one other point she, in common with the general public, also seemed unaware. The German and French Governments, recognising the fact that the presence of white women in their colonies does more than anything else to destroy abuses, raise the standard of morals, and make men contented with their lot, defray the cost of the voyage for the wife of every official, while the whole expense, averaging some seventy pounds per tour, must be borne by the Englishman, who, when all things are taken into account, is no more highly paid than his brother officials across the border.

It is, of course, true that many women are unsuited for the hardships of life out here. Some, too, might possibly hinder work, either by seeking to interfere in so-called "government palavers" which by no means concern them, or by holding back their husbands from that constant travelling which alone makes possible efficient supervision in countries such as these. For an official the interests of Government should naturally come before all others, but it would be easy enough for the authorities to judge, from travelling returns and district reports, whether, in any case, the presence of a wife had resulted in a falling off in efficiency, and those women deemed undesirable could be forbidden to return.

On behalf of my sister and myself I would venture to express thanks to Government for having allowed us, during nearly six years, to accompany my husband on all his journeyings. The conditions under which administration is carried on in countries such as this can hardly be grasped at home. In the chief towns it is true that, save for the unhealthiness of the climate, the state of affairs would not seem so much harder than in England; but in disturbed districts and at bush stations, where adequate supervision often entails ten to twelve hours work a day for long stretches, with the thermometer at a temperature of 80° to 90°, interspersed with marches varying from twelve to twenty miles per them in a downpour almost constant for nearly half the year, things wear a very different aspect. Under these conditions it is impossible for the overworked officials to give time to seemingly insignificant matters which are, however, so important in a climate such as this, i.e. variety of diet, food values, airing of garments, and, above all, the filtering of water. Were the restrictions now placed on the coming of wives removed, I venture to think it would do more than anything else to decrease the death toll and improve the standard of health in the tropics.

It was lately remarked to me by a woman of high rank in the colony, "Out here one hardly ever hears a man complain as to the worries and hardships of his lot." Difficulties are made light of and anxieties borne in silence, while on every hand one sees examples of devotion to duty not the less heroic because unrecorded, and a gay-hearted courage which is beyond all praise. Few even among the great Elizabethans took more terrible risks than are borne every day by one or other of these quiet men whose names are seldom or never heard in England. Yet, when in carrying out orders they meet a cruel death, as only too often happens, or still more frequently are invalided home, ruined in health by the hardship of life out here, scarcely a word of praise or thanks is accorded them.

At the present time, Nigeria is fortunate in the presence of a woman whose goodness, charm and broad sympathies are gratefully acknowledged by all who have the privilege of meeting her. Could but a few more such be attracted to the colony conditions would indeed soon show a vast improvement.

In conclusion, I would venture to add that, to the great anthropologists at home and to those highly placed officials who have given encouragement so unstinted, as also to the one whose selflessness made possible the writing of this little record, I have no words in which to express my grateful thanks. Had the idea been earlier suggested, or had it been possible before beginning to gather information concerning the women dealt with in these pages, to have had the advice of those scientists who on our return so generously devoted time and trouble to pointing out the best lines on which to carry out such a study, this little account would naturally have been of far greater value. We can only hope that--better equipped as we now are for further investigations, through the teaching and advice so more than kindly expended upon us--we may have the opportunity of undertaking fresh inquiries as to the women of other Nigerian tribes.

ENDNOTES

[1] "Sex Antagonism," p. 80. (p. 2)

[2] Die Pangwe. Völkerkundliche Monographie eines westafrikanischen Negerstammes. Von Gunter Tessmann. Vol. ii. (p. 5)

[3] "The difficulties to be overcome in general before I obtained even a glimpse into the secrets of male cults I have left to the imagination of the reader. With regard to feminine cults. these difficulties were so increased, through the exclusion of the male sex and the natural timidity of woman, that it was impossible for me to gain personal access to such." (p. 6)

[4] "In the Shadow of the Bush," p. 49. P. Amaury Talbot. (p. 13)

[5] "Magic and Fetishism," pp. 66-7. Dr. Haddon, F.R.S. (p. 14)

[6] Edinburgh Review," July, 1914. P. Amaury Talbot. (p. 14)

[7] "By Haunted Waters." P. Amaury Talbot--to be published shortly. (p. 16)

[8] "Osiris and the Egyptian Resurrection," p. 216. Dr. E. Wallis Budge. (p. 16)

[9] By Haunted Waters." P. Amaury Talbot. (p. 17)

[10] "Magic and Fetishism," p. 13. A. C. Haddon, F.R.S. (p. 18)

[11] "Volksthümlicher Brauch und Glaube bei Geburt und Taufe im Siebenburger Sachsenlande," p. 15. J. Hillner. (p. 19)

[12] Taboo and the Perils of the Soul," p. 294. J. G. Frazer. (p. 19)

[13] "The Devils and Evil Spirits of Babylonia." R. C. Thompson. Vol. i., p. xxvi. See also "Burial Customs." (p. 24)

[14] He proved to be a new species, and was named galago talbotti, by the British Museum authorities. (p. 38)

[15] The Religion of Ancient Egypt," pp. 108-9. Sayce. (p. 41)

[16] Among Ibos, however, whom we are at present studying, no such reluctance appears to be shown. A man, who believes himself possessed of the power to take on animal form, appears proud of this uncanny prerogative. (p. 44)

[17] Mimbo = palm wine. (p. 44)

[18] "In the Shadow of the Bush," pp. 133, 134, 136. P. Amaury Talbot. (p. 49)

[19] Maxwell in Straits Branch, Journal of the Royal Asiatic Society, No. 7, p. 26. (p. 53)

[20] Journal of the African Society, April, 1914, p. 248. (p. 73)

[21] Second Series, No. 12. (p. 89)

[22] A similar ceremony is carried out by Efik women in a holy water near Creek Town, which is thought to be sacred to a juju very powerful for the protection of women in childbirth. (p. 91)

[23] See p. 149. (p. 93)

[24] "By Haunted Waters." P. Amaury Talbot. (p. 114)

[25] Only a few years ago one of the present Provincial Commissioners, Mr. R. A. Roberts, in passing through the Eket district, came across one of these sad sacrifices set up by the roadside. (p. 115)

[26] "Fine Flowers in the Valley." (p. 116)

[27] Sir Hugh Clifford. (p. 137)

[28] Sir Hugh Clifford, "In Court and Kampong," pp. 230 and 244. (p. 139)

[29] Cf. the Malay custom of sprinkling "tepong tawar," which properly means "the neutralising rice-flour water," neutralising being used almost in a chemical sense, i.e. in the sense of "sterilising" the active element of poisons. A. E. Crawley, "Mystic Rose," p. 326. (p. 142)

[30] "Magic and Fetishism." (p. 154)

[31] "Magic and Fetishism," p. 12. A. C. Haddon, F.R.S. (p. 172)

[32] A full description of the ceremony of "recalling the Egbo" will be found under the heading "Burial Rites" in my husband's book "By Haunted Waters." (p. 173)

[33] "In the Shadow of the Bush," pp. 43-4. (Heinemann, London; George Doran, New York.) (p. 173)

[34] A full account of this terrible society will be found in "By Haunted Waters." (p. 174)

[35] "By Haunted Waters." P. Amaury Talbot. (p. 179)

[36] "Les Origines du Mariage et de la Famille," p. 448. Giraud Teulon. (p. 179)

[37] Edinburgh Review, July, 1914. P. Amaury Talbot. (p. 180)

[38] Journ. Anthrop. Inst., xxii., 111-12. J. Macdonald. (p. 181)

[39] "By Haunted Waters." P. Amaury Talbot. (p. 183)

[40] Since writing the above, it has been our good fortune to have the opportunity of studying the customs of Ibo and New Calabari women. It would seem that the lives of these latter are ruled, even more markedly than those of their Ibibio sisters, by rites of which nothing may be revealed to the males of the tribe, or indeed, to any man.

As an instance may be mentioned the secret rites carried out by every New Calabari widow during the seven days of mourning following the death of her husband. These strange ceremonies entail almost incredible self-denial, pain and discomfort on the unfortunate celebrants, but, according to unanimous testimony, no word of what transpires on such occasions has as yet reached male ears. (p. 186)

[41] "The Baganda, their Customs and Beliefs," p. 125. Roscoe. (p. 190)

[42] Devils and Evil Spirits of Babylonia." R. C. Thompson. (p. 191)

[43] "The Ballad of Clerk Saunders." (p. 192)

[44] Aymonier, quoted in "The Mystic Rose," p. 95. A. E. Crawley. (p. 193)

[45] "By Haunted Waters." P. Amaury Talbot. (p. 199)

[46] A full description of the obsequies of Iboibo chiefs will be found in my husband's book, "By Haunted Waters." Only so much as directly concerns the women is attempted here. (p. 205)

[47] Mr. W. W. Eakin, of the Kwa Ibo Mission. (p. 205)

[48] We could learn no reason for this last, seemingly inconsequent, tabu. (p. 205)

[49] A matter of much interest at the time of writing, but now relegated to the half-forgotten things of yesterday by the cataclysm which burst upon the world in August, 1914. (p. 213)

www.ingramcontent.com/pod-product-compliance
Lightning Source LLC
Chambersburg PA
CBHW051244020426
42333CB00025B/3051